Table Of Contents

Section 7: Deployment and Maintenance

Appendices

- Appendix A: WordPress Security Checklist
- Appendix B: Common Hooks (Actions & Filters) Quick Reference
- Appendix C: Deployment Checklist for Large-Scale Projects
- Appendix D: Resources for Further Learning

~ Conclusion

Disclaimer

This book is an independent resource and is not officially affiliated with, endorsed by, or sponsored by any company, organization, or trademark holder referenced within. All trademarks, service marks, product names, and company names or logos mentioned are the property of their respective owners. Use of these names or terms is solely for identification and reference purposes, and no association or endorsement by the respective trademark holder is implied. The content of this book is based on publicly available information, the author's research, and personal insights. This book is intended for educational and informational purposes only.

Welcome & What You'll Learn

Welcome to *WordPress for Professionals: Mastering Custom Themes and Plugins*

WordPress has come a long way from being a simple blogging tool to a robust, highly customizable content management system (CMS) that powers over 40% of the web. Whether you are a seasoned developer looking to refine your skills or a professional aiming to deepen your understanding of custom themes and plugins, this book will serve as a comprehensive guide to mastering advanced WordPress development.

This book is not for beginners. Instead, it is designed for web developers, freelancers, and agencies who already have foundational WordPress knowledge and want to take their expertise to the next level. We will explore intricate technical concepts, professional development workflows, and best practices that ensure high-quality, scalable, and secure WordPress solutions.

Why Master Custom Themes and Plugins?

Custom themes and plugins allow you to break free from pre-built solutions and tailor WordPress to meet unique project requirements. Whether you're building enterprise-level applications, optimizing performance, or extending WordPress beyond its default capabilities, mastering these two areas will empower you to create professional-grade digital experiences.

By the end of this book, you will be able to:

- Develop high-performance, fully customized themes tailored to specific business needs.
- Build custom plugins that extend WordPress functionality without bloating the system.
- Leverage the WordPress REST API and WP-CLI for automation and modern development workflows.
- Implement advanced security and performance optimization techniques.
- Work with cutting-edge technologies like React for building Gutenberg blocks and headless WordPress solutions.
- Adopt industry best practices for writing scalable, maintainable, and well-documented code.

What You'll Learn in This Book

This book is structured into seven sections, each focusing on a crucial aspect of professional WordPress development.

Section 1: Setting Up Your Development Environment

Before diving into development, we will cover the essential tools and configurations needed for a professional workflow. This includes setting up a local WordPress environment, configuring PHP and MySQL, debugging tools, and version control with Git.

Section 2: WordPress Fundamentals for Professionals

Understanding the inner workings of WordPress is crucial for professional development. We will explore WordPress architecture, the template hierarchy, and the WordPress REST API to prepare you for advanced customizations.

Section 3: Building Custom Themes from Scratch

This section provides a deep dive into WordPress theme development. You will learn about theme file structures, custom page templates, dynamic content management, responsive design principles, and performance optimization.

Section 4: Developing Custom Plugins

We will explore plugin development from the ground up, covering best practices, hooks, custom post types, form handling, AJAX integration, and plugin security.

Section 5: Advanced Theme and Plugin Techniques

This section covers advanced development concepts, such as combining themes and plugins for modular design, creating custom Gutenberg blocks using React, extending the WordPress dashboard, and integrating headless WordPress solutions.

Section 6: Best Practices for Professional Workflows

Writing efficient, maintainable code is key to professional development. Here, we will discuss OOP vs. procedural PHP, security hardening, performance optimization, accessibility standards, and proper documentation techniques.

Section 7: Deployment and Maintenance

Finally, we will cover deployment strategies, update management, backup solutions, and scalability techniques to ensure your WordPress projects remain secure and high-performing in a live environment.

Who This Book is For

This book is for:

- **WordPress developers** who want to move beyond theme and plugin customization and start building from scratch.
- **Freelancers and agencies** looking to offer custom WordPress solutions to clients.
- **Developers transitioning from other platforms** who want to understand how WordPress can be extended and optimized.
- **Tech professionals** who need an in-depth guide to advanced WordPress workflows and best practices.

How to Get the Most Out of This Book

- **Follow along with hands-on examples**: The best way to learn is by doing. Each chapter includes practical exercises, so set up a local development environment and code along.
- **Experiment beyond the examples**: Real-world projects often require creative problem-solving. Modify the code, test different configurations, and push your limits.
- **Adopt best practices**: Writing clean, maintainable, and scalable code is essential for professional development. Apply the best practices discussed in each chapter.
- **Engage with the WordPress community**: The WordPress ecosystem thrives on collaboration. Contribute to open-source projects, engage in forums, and stay updated with the latest advancements.

Let's Get Started

WordPress development is a constantly evolving field, and mastering custom themes and plugins will set you apart as a professional. Whether you are developing enterprise solutions, optimizing performance, or contributing to the open-source community, the knowledge in this book will give you the tools to create powerful and scalable WordPress applications.

Let's dive in and take your WordPress development skills to the next level!

Section 1:
Setting Up Your Development Environment

Installing WordPress Locally: Tools and Best Practices

Developing WordPress locally offers several advantages, including:

- **Faster development**: No need to constantly upload files to a remote server.
- **No internet dependency**: You can work without an internet connection.
- **Secure testing**: Experiment with themes and plugins without affecting a live website.
- **Efficient debugging**: Errors can be identified and fixed without exposing them to users.

A local environment mimics a live server, allowing you to test WordPress configurations, theme development, and plugin customizations in a controlled setting before deployment.

Choosing a Local Development Environment

To run WordPress locally, you need a web server, a database, and PHP. Several tools provide a bundled solution, making it easier to set up a local WordPress environment.

1. Local by Flywheel

- **Best for**: Beginners and advanced developers who need an easy-to-use yet powerful environment.
- **Key Features**:
    - One-click WordPress installation.
    - Built-in SSL support for HTTPS testing.
    - Easy switching between PHP versions.
    - Supports multiple local WordPress sites.
    - Live links for sharing projects with clients.

2. XAMPP (Windows, macOS, Linux)

- **Best for**: Developers who prefer manual control over their setup.
- **Key Features**:
    - Apache, MySQL (MariaDB), and PHP bundled together.
    - Open-source and widely supported.
    - Requires manual setup of virtual hosts for multiple sites.

3. MAMP (macOS, Windows)

- **Best for**: macOS users and those needing a simple GUI-based server.
- **Key Features**:
    - Apache, MySQL, and PHP pre-configured.
    - Easily switch PHP versions.
    - Comes with a Pro version for advanced features.

4. DevKinsta (Windows, macOS, Linux)

- **Best for**: Developers who need Docker-based WordPress environments.
- **Key Features**:
  - Free tool for setting up WordPress with Nginx, MySQL, and Redis.
  - Built-in mail-catching for testing emails.
  - Works seamlessly with Kinsta hosting.

5. Docker with WordPress

- **Best for**: Developers who want an isolated, version-controlled environment.
- **Key Features**:
  - Runs WordPress in containers, ensuring environment consistency.
  - Ideal for team collaboration and CI/CD workflows.
  - Requires knowledge of Docker Compose.

Installing WordPress Locally Using Local by Flywheel (Recommended for Most Developers)

1. **Download Local by Flywheel**
   - Visit [localwp.com] (https://localwp.com/) and download the installer for your OS.
2. **Install and Launch Local**
   - Follow the installation instructions and open Local.
3. **Create a New Site**
   - Click **"Create a New Site"** and enter a site name.
   - Choose **Preferred** or **Custom** environment.
   - Set up your WordPress username and password.
4. **Start the Local Server**
   - Click **Start Site**, and Local will handle the setup.
   - Click **Admin** to log into the WordPress dashboard.
5. **Test the Site**
   - Your local site will be available at a `.local` domain (e.g., `http://mysite.local`).
6. **Enable SSL for HTTPS Testing**
   - Click **Trust** next to the SSL option in Local settings.

Installing WordPress Manually with XAMPP

For developers who prefer more control, setting up WordPress manually with XAMPP is a good alternative.

Step 1: Download and Install XAMPP

- Download XAMPP from [apachefriends.org] (https://www.apachefriends.org/) and install it.
- Open the XAMPP Control Panel and start **Apache** and **MySQL**.

Step 2: Download WordPress

- Visit [wordpress.org] (https://wordpress.org/download/) and download the latest version.
- Extract the WordPress files into `C:\xampp\htdocs\mysite` (Windows) or `/Applications/XAMPP/htdocs/mysite` (macOS).

Step 3: Create a Database

- Open http://localhost/phpmyadmin in your browser.

- Click **Databases** > **Create Database** > Name it mysite_db > Click **Create**.

Step 4: Configure WordPress

- Go to http://localhost/mysite in your browser.
- Choose a language and enter database details:
  - Database Name: mysite_db
  - Username: root
  - Password: (leave blank)
  - Host: localhost
- Click **Submit** and complete the WordPress installation.

Best Practices for Local WordPress Development

1. Use Version Control (Git)

- Track changes to your themes and plugins using Git.
- Use .gitignore to exclude files like wp-config.php and wp-content/uploads/.

2. Enable Debugging for Development

Add the following to wp-config.php:

```
define('WP_DEBUG', true);
define('WP_DEBUG_LOG', true);
define('WP_DEBUG_DISPLAY', false);
@ini_set('display_errors', 0);
```

This ensures errors are logged in wp-content/debug.log instead of being displayed on the screen.

3. Work with WP-CLI for Efficiency

- WP-CLI allows you to manage WordPress via the command line.
- Install WP-CLI and use commands like:

```
wp plugin install woocommerce --activate
wp theme install astra --activate
wp user create admin admin@example.com --role=administrator
```

4. Keep Your Environment Updated

- Use the latest versions of PHP, MySQL, and WordPress to match modern hosting environments.
- Test your themes and plugins against upcoming WordPress releases using [WordPress Beta Tester] (https://wordpress.org/plugins/wordpress-beta-tester/).

5. Optimize Performance

- Increase PHP memory limit in wp-config.php:

```
define('WP_MEMORY_LIMIT', '256M');
```

- Use caching plugins like WP Super Cache for better speed testing.

6. Secure Your Local Environment

- Change default database prefixes from wp_ to something unique.
- Use strong admin passwords, even in local development.
- Restrict access to wp-config.php:

```
<Files wp-config.php>
order allow,deny
deny from all
</Files>
```

Summary

Installing WordPress locally is a crucial step in professional development workflows. Whether you use a tool like **Local by Flywheel** for an easy setup or **XAMPP** for more control, having a local environment helps streamline development, debugging, and testing. By following best practices such as **using version control, enabling debugging, and optimizing performance**, you can ensure your local setup mirrors a professional live environment.

With WordPress installed and configured locally, you are now ready to dive into advanced development techniques. In the next chapter, we will explore **configuring PHP, MySQL, and debugging tools** to fine-tune your environment for optimal performance.

Configuring PHP, MySQL, and Debugging Tools

A well-configured development environment is essential for professional WordPress development. In this chapter, we will cover how to configure **PHP**, **MySQL**, and essential **debugging tools** to ensure a smooth development workflow. Proper configurations improve performance, security, and debugging efficiency, making your development process more reliable and efficient.

Configuring PHP for WordPress

PHP is the backbone of WordPress, handling everything from database interactions to template rendering. By optimizing PHP settings, you can enhance performance and compatibility for local development.

1. Setting the Correct PHP Version

WordPress recommends using **PHP 8.0 or later** for better performance and security. You can check your current PHP version using:

```
php -v
```

To switch PHP versions:

- **Local by Flywheel**: Change the PHP version from the site's settings.
- **XAMPP/MAMP**: Download the desired PHP version and configure it in the settings.
- **Docker**: Update the PHP container in `docker-compose.yml`.

2. Updating PHP Configuration (php.ini)

Modify the `php.ini` file to optimize WordPress development. The location of `php.ini` varies:

- **XAMPP**: `C:\xampp\php\php.ini`
- **MAMP**: `/Applications/MAMP/bin/php/phpX.X.X/conf/php.ini`
- **Linux/macOS**: Run `php --ini` to find the location.

Recommended settings:

```
memory_limit = 256M
upload_max_filesize = 64M
post_max_size = 64M
max_execution_time = 300
display_errors = On
log_errors = On
error_log = /var/log/php_errors.log
```

These settings increase memory for WordPress, allow larger file uploads, and enable error logging for debugging.

3. Installing PHP Extensions

Ensure these PHP extensions are enabled:

- `mysqli` – Required for MySQL database interaction.
- `mbstring` – Handles multibyte string encoding.
- `curl` – Used for external API requests.
- `gd` – Image processing.

- opcache – Performance optimization.

Check enabled extensions using:

```
php -m
```

To install missing extensions:

- **Ubuntu/Debian**:

    ```
    sudo apt install php-mysql php-mbstring php-curl php-gd php-opcache
    ```

- **Mac (Homebrew)**:

    ```
    brew install php
    ```

Configuring MySQL for WordPress

MySQL is the default database system for WordPress. Proper configuration ensures efficient data storage, retrieval, and security.

1. Setting Up MySQL Database

For local development, create a database using:

Using phpMyAdmin (XAMPP, MAMP, Local by Flywheel):

1. Open http://localhost/phpmyadmin.
2. Click **Databases** > **Create Database** > Name it wordpress_dev.

Using MySQL CLI:

```
mysql -u root -p
CREATE DATABASE wordpress_dev;
```

2. Configuring MySQL for Better Performance

Modify my.cnf or my.ini (MySQL configuration file) to optimize performance.

File locations:

- **Windows (XAMPP/MAMP):** C:\xampp\mysql\bin\my.ini
- **Linux/macOS:** /etc/mysql/my.cnf

Recommended settings:

```
max_allowed_packet = 64M
innodb_buffer_pool_size = 256M
query_cache_size = 64M
slow_query_log = 1
slow_query_log_file = /var/log/mysql_slow_queries.log
```

These settings optimize query performance and enable slow query logging to help debug inefficient queries.

3. Managing MySQL with WP-CLI

WP-CLI provides an efficient way to interact with the WordPress database.

Example Commands:

- **Create a new database user**:

```
wp db create --user=root --password=root
```

- **Optimize the database**:

```
wp db optimize
```

- **Run database queries**:

```
wp db query "SELECT * FROM wp_users;"
```

Setting Up Debugging Tools

Debugging is an essential part of professional development. WordPress provides built-in debugging tools, and third-party tools can enhance troubleshooting capabilities.

1. Enabling WordPress Debug Mode

Enable debugging in `wp-config.php` by adding:

```
define('WP_DEBUG', true);
define('WP_DEBUG_LOG', true);
define('WP_DEBUG_DISPLAY', false);
@ini_set('display_errors', 0);
```

This logs errors to `wp-content/debug.log` without displaying them on the site.

2. Debugging Database Queries

Enable query debugging to inspect SQL queries:

```
define('SAVEQUERIES', true);
define('WP_DEBUG', true);
```

View queries using:

```
global $wpdb;
print_r($wpdb->queries);
```

3. Using Query Monitor Plugin

[Query Monitor] (https://wordpress.org/plugins/query-monitor/) is a powerful plugin that provides:

- Slow query detection.
- PHP errors and warnings.
- Hooks and filters tracking.

Install via WP-CLI:

```
wp plugin install query-monitor --activate
```

4. Xdebug for Advanced PHP Debugging

[Xdebug] (https://xdebug.org/) is a PHP extension that enables step-through debugging with IDEs like **VS Code** and **PHPStorm**.

Installation:

- **Ubuntu**:

```
sudo apt install php-xdebug
```

- **Mac (Homebrew)**:

```
pecl install xdebug
```

Enable Xdebug in php.ini:

```
zend_extension=xdebug.so
xdebug.mode=debug
xdebug.start_with_request=yes
xdebug.client_host=127.0.0.1
xdebug.client_port=9003
```

To verify installation:

```
php -m | grep xdebug
```

Configuring VS Code for Xdebug:

1. Install the **PHP Debug** extension.
2. Create .vscode/launch.json:

```
{
  "version": "0.2.0",
  "configurations": [
    {
      "name": "Listen for Xdebug",
      "type": "php",
      "request": "launch",
      "port": 9003
    }
  ]
}
```

Start debugging with breakpoints in VS Code.

Summary

A properly configured **PHP and MySQL environment** improves WordPress performance and security, while debugging tools like **WP_DEBUG, Query Monitor, and Xdebug** make troubleshooting efficient.

Key Takeaways:
✔ Use **PHP 8.0+** and adjust php.ini for better performance.
✔ Optimize **MySQL settings** for faster queries and improved caching.
✔ Enable **WordPress debugging** using WP_DEBUG_LOG.

✔ Use **Query Monitor** for tracking database performance.
✔ Integrate **Xdebug** for advanced PHP debugging in an IDE.

With these configurations in place, your development environment is now optimized for **efficient debugging and performance tuning**.

Version Control with Git for WordPress Projects

Version control is an essential part of modern software development, and **Git** is the industry-standard tool for tracking changes, collaborating with teams, and managing code efficiently. Whether you're working on custom themes, plugins, or even core WordPress modifications, implementing a **Git-based workflow** will help maintain code integrity, improve collaboration, and streamline deployment.

In this chapter, we will cover:

- Why Git is essential for WordPress development
- Setting up Git for a WordPress project
- Using Git commands for version control
- Best practices for managing WordPress themes and plugins with Git
- Working with remote repositories like GitHub, GitLab, and Bitbucket

---

Why Use Git for WordPress Development?

Using Git in WordPress development provides several benefits:

✔ **Track Changes** – Easily revert to previous versions of your code.
✔ **Collaboration** – Work with teams without overwriting each other's changes.
✔ **Branching & Merging** – Develop new features without disrupting the main project.
✔ **Safe Deployments** – Push tested changes to production environments.
✔ **Backup & Recovery** – Protect your code from accidental loss or corruption.

Whether you're a solo developer or part of a team, using Git ensures a structured and reliable approach to WordPress development.

Installing Git and Setting Up a Repository

Before using Git, ensure it is installed on your system.

1. Installing Git

Windows: Download and install Git from [git-scm.com] (https://git-scm.com/). During installation, choose **Git Bash** for a command-line interface.

macOS: Install Git using Homebrew:

```
brew install git
```

Linux (Debian/Ubuntu):

```
sudo apt install git
```

To verify the installation, run:

```
git --version
```

2. Configuring Git

Set up your name and email for commit tracking:

```
git config --global user.name "Your Name"
```

```
git config --global user.email "your.email@example.com"
```

Check your configuration with:

```
git config --list
```

3. Initializing a Git Repository in a WordPress Project

Navigate to your local WordPress project directory and initialize Git:

```
cd /path/to/your/wordpress-project
git init
```

This creates a **.git** folder that stores all version history.

4. Adding and Committing Files

To track all files in the project:

```
git add .
git commit -m "Initial commit - WordPress project setup"
```

Best Practices for Managing WordPress Projects with Git

Using Git effectively in WordPress requires thoughtful organization. Here's how to structure your project for optimal Git usage:

1. Using a .gitignore File

WordPress generates many temporary and non-essential files that shouldn't be tracked in Git. Create a **.gitignore** file in the root directory to exclude unnecessary files:

```
# Ignore WordPress core files
wordpress/
wp-config.php
wp-content/uploads/
wp-content/backup/
wp-content/cache/

# Ignore system files
.DS_Store
Thumbs.db
node_modules/
vendor/
.env
```

To commit only your theme or plugin:

```
git add wp-content/themes/your-theme
git commit -m "Added custom theme files"
```

2. Working with Feature Branches

Instead of making changes directly on the **main** branch, use branches:

- Create a new feature branch:

```
git checkout -b feature-custom-header
```

- Make changes, then commit:

```
git add .
git commit -m "Added custom header section"
```

- Merge back to the main branch:

```
git checkout main
git merge feature-custom-header
```

Using branches ensures **clean and organized development workflows**.

3. Using Git Hooks for Automation

Git hooks help automate tasks. For example, a **pre-commit hook** can check for syntax errors before allowing a commit.

Create a file in .git/hooks/pre-commit:

```
#!/bin/sh
php -l wp-content/themes/your-theme/functions.php
```

Make it executable:

```
chmod +x .git/hooks/pre-commit
```

Now, Git will reject commits with PHP syntax errors.

Using Remote Repositories (GitHub, GitLab, Bitbucket)

Using a remote repository allows you to store and collaborate on your code.

1. Creating a Remote Repository

On **GitHub/GitLab/Bitbucket**, create a new repository (without initializing it). Then, link your local project:

```
git remote add origin https://github.com/yourusername/your-repository.git
git push -u origin main
```

2. Cloning a WordPress Repository

To clone an existing WordPress project:

```
git clone https://github.com/yourusername/your-repository.git
cd your-repository
```

3. Pushing and Pulling Changes

After making changes, push them to the remote repository:

```
git push origin main
```

To update your local copy with the latest changes:

```
git pull origin main
```

Deploying WordPress Projects with Git

Git can streamline deployment to staging or production environments.

1. Deploying Using Git Hooks

On the remote server, create a `post-receive` hook:

```
#!/bin/sh
GIT_WORK_TREE=/var/www/html/wordpress git checkout -f
```

Save it in `.git/hooks/post-receive` and make it executable:

```
chmod +x .git/hooks/post-receive
```

Now, when you push to the server, the WordPress project updates automatically.

2. Deploying via GitHub Actions

GitHub Actions automates deployment. Add a `.github/workflows/deploy.yml` file:

```yaml
name: Deploy to Server

on:
  push:
    branches:
      - main

jobs:
  deploy:
    runs-on: ubuntu-latest
    steps:
      - name: Checkout Repository
        uses: actions/checkout@v2

      - name: Deploy to Server
        run: |
          ssh user@server 'cd /var/www/html && git pull origin main'
```

Every push to `main` triggers automatic deployment.

Summary

Using Git for WordPress development **improves project management, collaboration, and deployment efficiency**. By tracking code changes, working with branches, and using remote repositories, you can **ensure a structured and reliable workflow**.

✔ **Use Git to track custom themes and plugins.**
✔ **Set up a .gitignore file to exclude unnecessary files.**
✔ **Use feature branches for new developments.**

✔ **Leverage Git hooks for automation and error checking.**
✔ **Deploy changes via Git push or GitHub Actions.**

With Git integrated into your workflow, your WordPress development process will be more **efficient, organized, and scalable**.

Section 2:
WordPress Fundamentals for Professionals

Understanding the WordPress Architecture

To master WordPress development, it is essential to understand its architecture. WordPress is built on a **modular and extensible framework**, making it one of the most flexible content management systems (CMS) available.

In this chapter, we will explore:

- The **core components** of WordPress
- How **the request lifecycle** works
- The **database structure** and how WordPress stores data
- How themes and plugins interact with the **WordPress core**

Understanding these fundamentals will help you create optimized themes and plugins while maintaining **scalability, security, and best practices**.

Core Components of WordPress

WordPress consists of four main components:

1. WordPress Core

- The **core files** of WordPress provide its essential functionality.
- These include PHP scripts that handle routing, content management, and API requests.
- **Never modify core files** directly, as updates will overwrite them.

2. Themes

- Themes control the **visual presentation** of a WordPress site.
- They consist of **PHP, HTML, CSS, and JavaScript** files that dictate layout and design.
- Custom themes allow full control over a site's appearance and functionality.

3. Plugins

- Plugins **extend the functionality** of WordPress.
- They can add custom post types, integrations, and features like SEO optimization or security enhancements.
- Well-developed plugins use **WordPress hooks (actions & filters)** to interact with core functions.

4. Database

- Stores all WordPress content, including **posts, pages, users, and settings**.
- Uses MySQL (or MariaDB) as the database management system.
- Efficient database queries are critical for performance optimization.

Each of these components works together through **WordPress hooks and APIs**, enabling developers to customize and extend functionality.

The WordPress Request Lifecycle

Understanding the **request lifecycle** helps in debugging issues, optimizing performance, and building efficient plugins/themes.

1. User Requests a Page

When a visitor accesses a WordPress page, a request is sent to the server.
For example, visiting `https://example.com/about` triggers a request to the server to fetch the **About page** content.

2. The WordPress Index.php File is Executed

All requests in WordPress are routed through `index.php`, which loads the WordPress environment.

3. Loading the wp-config.php File

- `wp-config.php` contains the **database connection details**.
- WordPress reads this file to determine how to interact with the database.

4. The Database is Queried

- WordPress fetches content from the **wp_posts** table and other related tables.
- Query results are passed through **template files** to generate the page.

5. The Theme is Loaded

- Based on the **template hierarchy**, WordPress selects the appropriate PHP file.
- Example: If a user visits a blog post, `single.php` or `single-post.php` is loaded.

6. WordPress Hooks are Triggered

- Actions and filters allow themes and plugins to **modify the request and response**.
- Example: A caching plugin might modify the response to serve a cached version instead of running new queries.

7. The Final HTML is Rendered and Sent to the Browser

- The PHP code executes, retrieves data, and outputs **HTML, CSS, and JavaScript** to the browser.
- The user sees the final web page.

Understanding the WordPress Database Structure

The WordPress database is structured with **12 core tables**, each serving a specific function.

Table Name	Purpose
wp_posts	Stores posts, pages, and custom post types.
wp_postmeta	Stores metadata (custom fields) related to posts.
wp_users	Stores registered user data.

wp_usermeta	Stores user-related metadata.
wp_options	Stores site settings and plugin configurations.
wp_comments	Stores comments made on posts and pages.
wp_commentmeta	Stores metadata for comments.
wp_terms	Stores categories, tags, and custom taxonomies.
wp_term_taxonomy	Defines relationships between terms and taxonomies.
wp_term_relationships	Links terms to posts or custom post types.
wp_links	Stores links for the now-deprecated WordPress Links feature.
wp_meta	Stores metadata about database objects.

Common Queries for WordPress Development

Retrieve the latest 5 published posts:

```
SELECT * FROM wp_posts WHERE post_status = 'publish' AND post_type = 'post'
ORDER BY post_date DESC LIMIT 5;
```

Count the total number of users:

```
SELECT COUNT(*) FROM wp_users;
```

Get all custom meta fields for a specific post:

```
SELECT meta_key, meta_value FROM wp_postmeta WHERE post_id = 123;
```

Understanding these queries is essential when optimizing performance and customizing WordPress features.

How Themes and Plugins Interact with the WordPress Core

Both themes and plugins rely on **WordPress APIs** to modify or extend default behavior.

1. Theme Integration

- Themes use **template files** and **functions.php** to structure content.
- The **Template Hierarchy** determines which file is used to display content.

Example: A **single post** request loads one of the following files in order:

1. single-{post-type}.php
2. single.php
3. index.php

2. Plugin Integration

- Plugins use **hooks (actions & filters)** to modify core behavior without altering WordPress files.

- Example: Adding content before a post using the `the_content` filter.

```
function add_before_post_content($content) {
    if (is_single()) {
        return '<p>Custom message before post content</p>' . $content;
    }
    return $content;
}
add_filter('the_content', 'add_before_post_content');
```

3. API Integration

WordPress provides several APIs for extending functionality:

- **WP REST API** – Enables headless WordPress and external integrations.
- **Shortcode API** – Allows embedding dynamic content in posts/pages.
- **Widgets API** – Custom widgets for sidebars and footers.
- **WP_Query API** – Retrieves custom post queries efficiently.

Example: Query the latest 3 blog posts using `WP_Query`:

```
$args = array(
    'post_type' => 'post',
    'posts_per_page' => 3
);
$custom_query = new WP_Query($args);
while ($custom_query->have_posts()) : $custom_query->the_post();
    the_title('<h2>', '</h2>');
    the_excerpt();
endwhile;
wp_reset_postdata();
```

These APIs allow developers to build **powerful, flexible, and maintainable** WordPress applications.

Summary

Understanding the **WordPress architecture** is crucial for professional development.

✔ **WordPress Core** handles all essential functions.
✔ **The Request Lifecycle** explains how WordPress processes user requests.
✔ **The Database Structure** stores content, users, metadata, and settings.
✔ **Themes and Plugins** modify WordPress via template files and hooks.
✔ **APIs like WP_Query, REST API, and Shortcode API** enable powerful customizations.

With this foundation, you can now **build custom themes and plugins efficiently**, ensuring they integrate smoothly into the WordPress ecosystem.

The Template Hierarchy Demystified

The **WordPress Template Hierarchy** is a fundamental concept that determines how WordPress selects and displays templates for different types of content. Understanding the template hierarchy is essential for customizing themes efficiently and ensuring that the right files are used for rendering pages, posts, archives, and custom content types.

In this chapter, we will explore:

- How WordPress selects templates based on requests
- The hierarchy structure for different types of content
- How to override and customize template files
- Best practices for working with the template hierarchy

By mastering the template hierarchy, you will be able to **create custom themes** that dynamically adjust to different content types without unnecessary duplication.

Understanding the Template Hierarchy

The template hierarchy is a **system of fallback rules** that WordPress follows when determining which template file to load.

For example:

- If a visitor requests a **single post**, WordPress looks for `single-{post-type}.php`, then `single.php`, and finally `index.php`.
- If a visitor views a **category archive**, WordPress checks `category-{slug}.php`, then `category.php`, and finally `archive.php`.

This structured approach allows developers to **target specific types of content while keeping themes organized**.

How WordPress Determines Which Template to Use

When a user requests a page, WordPress follows these steps to select the appropriate template:

1. **Identifies the request type** (single post, page, archive, search, etc.).
2. **Looks for the most specific template file** based on the hierarchy.
3. **Falls back to more generic templates** if a specific file is missing.
4. **Uses index.php** as the ultimate fallback.

Breakdown of the WordPress Template Hierarchy

The hierarchy is divided into different content types:

1. Single Post Template Hierarchy

When a visitor views a single blog post, WordPress searches for templates in this order:

1. `single-{post-type}.php` – For custom post types (e.g., `single-product.php` for WooCommerce).
2. `single.php` – The generic template for all posts.

3. `index.php` – The final fallback.

Example:

If you have a custom post type `portfolio`, WordPress will first look for:

- `single-portfolio.php`
- If unavailable, it will use `single.php`.
- If `single.php` is also missing, it will default to `index.php`.

2. Page Template Hierarchy

When viewing a **static page**, WordPress follows this order:

1. `page-{slug}.php` – A custom template for a specific page (e.g., `page-about.php` for the About page).
2. `page-{id}.php` – Targets a page by its ID (e.g., `page-42.php`).
3. `page.php` – The generic page template.
4. `index.php` – The fallback.

Example:

If you have a page titled "Contact" with a slug of `contact`, WordPress will try to load:

1. `page-contact.php`
2. `page.php`
3. `index.php`

---

3. Category and Tag Archives

When viewing a **category or tag archive**, WordPress follows this order:

1. `category-{slug}.php` – For a specific category (e.g., `category-news.php`).
2. `category-{id}.php` – Targets a category by its ID (e.g., `category-3.php`).
3. `category.php` – The generic category template.
4. `archive.php` – The fallback for all archive pages.
5. `index.php` – The ultimate fallback.

For **tags**, the hierarchy is similar:

1. `tag-{slug}.php`
2. `tag-{id}.php`
3. `tag.php`
4. `archive.php`
5. `index.php`

---

4. Custom Post Types and Taxonomies

When using **custom post types** and **custom taxonomies**, WordPress follows this order:

Single Custom Post Type:

1. `single-{custom-post-type}.php`

2. `single.php`
3. `index.php`

Custom Taxonomy Archive:

1. `taxonomy-{taxonomy}-{slug}.php`
2. `taxonomy-{taxonomy}.php`
3. `archive.php`
4. `index.php`

Example:

For a custom post type `books` and a custom taxonomy `genre`, WordPress will look for:

- `single-books.php` → for single book entries.
- `taxonomy-genre-fiction.php` → for the "fiction" archive.

---

5. Other Common Templates

Template Type	Files WordPress Checks
Home Page	`home.php` → `index.php`
Front Page (Static Home)	`front-page.php` → `home.php` → `index.php`
Search Results	`search.php` → `index.php`
Author Archives	`author-{username}.php` → `author.php` → `archive.php` → `index.php`
Date Archives	`date.php` → `archive.php` → `index.php`
404 Error Page	`404.php` → `index.php`

Creating and Customizing Template Files

Now that we understand the hierarchy, let's create and modify templates.

1. Creating a Custom Page Template

To create a custom page layout, add a new file inside your theme's folder:

Example: Creating `page-contact.php`

```php
<?php
/*
Template Name: Contact Page
*/
get_header();
?>
<h1>Contact Us</h1>
<p>This is a custom template for the Contact page.</p>
<?php get_footer(); ?>
```

Then, assign the **Contact Page Template** to a specific page from the WordPress editor.

---

2. Customizing the Blog Homepage

If you want to design a custom homepage:

1. Create `front-page.php`.
2. Add a dynamic layout using `WP_Query`.

Example:

```php
<?php get_header(); ?>
<h1>Latest Posts</h1>
<?php
$query = new WP_Query(['posts_per_page' => 5]);
while ($query->have_posts()) : $query->the_post(); ?>
    <h2><a href="<?php the_permalink(); ?>"><?php the_title(); ?></a></h2>
    <p><?php the_excerpt(); ?></p>
<?php endwhile; ?>
<?php get_footer(); ?>
```

This overrides WordPress's default homepage with a **custom blog layout**.

Best Practices for Using the Template Hierarchy

✔ **Follow the hierarchy structure** to keep themes organized.
✔ **Use `get_template_part()`** to break templates into reusable parts.
✔ **Create custom templates** when needed, but avoid unnecessary duplication.
✔ **Use conditional tags** like `is_home()` and `is_category()` to control template logic dynamically.

Example: Adding a banner only to archive pages:

```php
if (is_archive()) {
    echo '<div class="archive-banner">Welcome to the Archives</div>';
}
```

Summary

The **WordPress Template Hierarchy** provides a structured way to determine which template files are used for different types of content.

✔ WordPress **follows a specific order** when selecting templates.
✔ **Custom templates** can be created for pages, posts, and archives.
✔ **Efficient template management** improves site performance and maintainability.
✔ **Best practices like using `get_template_part()` and conditional logic** help streamline development.

Mastering the template hierarchy will **empower you to build flexible, dynamic WordPress themes**.

Working with the WordPress REST API

The **WordPress REST API** is a powerful tool that allows developers to interact with WordPress data using HTTP requests. It enables seamless integration between WordPress and external applications, making it possible to build **headless WordPress sites, mobile apps, and third-party integrations**.

In this chapter, we will explore:

- What the **WordPress REST API** is and why it matters
- How to fetch data using REST API endpoints
- Creating custom REST API endpoints
- Authenticating API requests for security
- Practical use cases for integrating WordPress with external applications

By mastering the REST API, you can extend WordPress far beyond traditional themes and plugins.

What is the WordPress REST API?

The **REST API (Representational State Transfer Application Programming Interface)** provides a standardized way to access WordPress content using **JSON data format** over HTTP.

With the REST API, you can:

✔ Fetch posts, pages, comments, users, and custom content via **API endpoints**
✔ Create, update, and delete WordPress content programmatically
✔ Connect WordPress with **React, Vue.js, mobile apps, or third-party services**
✔ Build headless WordPress sites where the frontend is separate from the backend

By default, the REST API is **enabled in all modern WordPress installations**, allowing developers to retrieve content via simple HTTP requests.

Fetching Data Using REST API Endpoints

WordPress provides **default API endpoints** to access different types of content.

1. Retrieving Posts

To fetch all published posts, send a GET request to:

https://example.com/wp-json/wp/v2/posts

Example response (JSON format):

```
[
  {
    "id": 1,
    "title": {"rendered": "Hello World"},
    "content": {"rendered": "<p>Welcome to WordPress!</p>"},
    "link": "https://example.com/hello-world"
  }
]
```

2. Retrieving a Single Post

Fetch a post by its ID:

https://example.com/wp-json/wp/v2/posts/1

Fetch a post by its slug:

https://example.com/wp-json/wp/v2/posts?slug=hello-world

3. Fetching Categories and Tags

Retrieve all categories:

https://example.com/wp-json/wp/v2/categories

Retrieve all tags:

https://example.com/wp-json/wp/v2/tags

4. Retrieving Pages

To fetch all pages:

https://example.com/wp-json/wp/v2/pages

Creating Custom REST API Endpoints

While the default REST API endpoints cover basic content, sometimes you need **custom endpoints** to retrieve or manipulate specific data.

1. Registering a Custom Endpoint

Add the following code to your **theme's functions.php** or **a custom plugin**:

```
function my_custom_api_endpoint() {
    return new WP_REST_Response(['message' => 'Hello, API!'], 200);
}

function register_custom_route() {
    register_rest_route('custom/v1', '/hello', [
        'methods' => 'GET',
        'callback' => 'my_custom_api_endpoint'
    ]);
}

add_action('rest_api_init', 'register_custom_route');
```

Now, sending a GET request to:

https://example.com/wp-json/custom/v1/hello

Returns:

```
{"message": "Hello, API!"}
```

2. Fetching Custom Post Types via REST API

By default, the REST API does not expose **custom post types** unless explicitly enabled.

To make a **custom post type** REST-accessible, modify its registration:

```
register_post_type('portfolio', [
    'label' => 'Portfolio',
    'public' => true,
    'show_in_rest' => true
]);
```

Now, you can fetch **portfolio posts** via:

https://example.com/wp-json/wp/v2/portfolio

3. Adding Parameters to Custom Endpoints

Pass parameters like category or date filters:

```
function custom_posts_by_category($request) {
    $category = $request['category'];
    $posts = get_posts(['category_name' => $category, 'posts_per_page' => 5]);

    return rest_ensure_response($posts);
}

add_action('rest_api_init', function() {
    register_rest_route('custom/v1', '/posts/(?P<category>[a-zA-Z0-9-]+)', [
        'methods' => 'GET',
        'callback' => 'custom_posts_by_category'
    ]);
});
```

Now, requesting:

https://example.com/wp-json/custom/v1/posts/news

Retrieves the latest **5 posts from the "news" category**.

Securing REST API Requests

1. Public vs. Private Endpoints

- **Public endpoints** (e.g., fetching posts) require no authentication.
- **Private endpoints** (e.g., creating/updating posts) require authentication.

2. Authentication Methods

✔ **Cookie Authentication** (Default) – Used when logged into WordPress.
✔ **Application Passwords** – Secure method for third-party integrations.
✔ **OAuth or JWT Authentication** – Ideal for headless WordPress setups.

3. Using Application Passwords

Enable **Application Passwords** in WordPress and authenticate API requests:

```
curl --user "username:application-password" -X POST -d '{"title":"New Post"}' \
-H "Content-Type: application/json" https://example.com/wp-json/wp/v2/posts
```

This allows you to **create and update content securely**.

Practical Use Cases for the WordPress REST API

1. Creating a Headless WordPress Site

- Use WordPress as a **backend-only CMS** and build the frontend with **React, Vue.js, or Next.js**.
- Example: Fetch posts using JavaScript:

```
fetch('https://example.com/wp-json/wp/v2/posts')
  .then(response => response.json())
  .then(data => console.log(data));
```

2. Integrating WordPress with a Mobile App

- A mobile app (iOS/Android) can **fetch WordPress posts** using the REST API.
- Example: Display latest posts in a React Native app.

3. Automating Content Publishing

- Use **Zapier, IFTTT, or Node.js scripts** to publish posts automatically.
- Example: Auto-publish new blog posts when an external API event triggers.

4. Enhancing Search Functionality

- Customize REST API responses to **include custom metadata** for better search experiences.

Summary

The WordPress REST API enables developers to **interact with WordPress content programmatically**, making it possible to create headless sites, mobile apps, and external integrations.

✔ Fetch posts, pages, categories, and users using **default REST endpoints**.
✔ Create **custom API endpoints** to expose specific data.
✔ Secure API requests using **application passwords and authentication**.
✔ Integrate WordPress with **React, Vue.js, mobile apps, and automation tools**.

Mastering the REST API opens new possibilities for **modern WordPress development**.

Section 3:
Building Custom Themes from Scratch

Theme Structure: Files, Directories, and Naming Conventions

A well-structured theme is the foundation of professional WordPress development. Understanding the **theme structure, essential files, directories, and naming conventions** ensures that your themes are **organized, maintainable, and compatible** with WordPress standards.

In this chapter, we will cover:

- The **core structure** of a WordPress theme
- Essential **files and directories**
- Proper **naming conventions** for theme files
- How WordPress loads and prioritizes template files
- Best practices for structuring your theme

By mastering these principles, you will be able to **build custom themes from scratch that follow WordPress best practices** and remain easily extendable.

Understanding the WordPress Theme Structure

A WordPress theme consists of **a set of PHP, CSS, JavaScript, and image files** that determine how content is displayed on the front end.

Basic structure of a WordPress theme:

```
my-custom-theme/
|—— style.css
|—— functions.php
|—— index.php
|—— header.php
|—— footer.php
|—— sidebar.php
|—— page.php
|—— single.php
|—— archive.php
|—— search.php
|—— 404.php
|—— assets/
|   |—— css/
|   |—— js/
|   |—— images/
|—— template-parts/
|—— inc/
|—— languages/
|—— screenshot.png
```

Let's break down each component in detail.

Essential Theme Files and Their Functions

Each theme file serves a specific purpose in WordPress.

1. Required Theme Files

File	Purpose
style.css	Contains theme metadata and global styles.
functions.php	Adds custom functionality and hooks into WordPress.
index.php	Default fallback template if no other template is available.

Example: style.css

Every WordPress theme must have a **style.css** file with the following metadata at the top:

```
/*
Theme Name: My Custom Theme
Theme URI: https://example.com/
Author: Your Name
Author URI: https://example.com/
Description: A custom WordPress theme.
Version: 1.0
License: GNU General Public License v2 or later
License URI: https://www.gnu.org/licenses/gpl-2.0.html
Text Domain: my-custom-theme
*/
```

---

2. Core Template Files

File	Purpose
header.php	Contains the site's <head> section and opening <body>.
footer.php	Contains the closing <body> and <footer>.
sidebar.php	Defines the sidebar area (widgets, menus, etc.).
page.php	Displays static pages (e.g., About, Contact).
single.php	Displays individual blog posts.
archive.php	Handles category, tag, and custom post archives.
search.php	Displays search results.

`404.php`	Displays a custom error page when a page is not found.

3. The Functions.php File

`functions.php` acts as the **brain** of your theme, allowing you to:

✔ Register styles and scripts
✔ Add theme support (menus, widgets, thumbnails)
✔ Define custom post types and taxonomies
✔ Modify WordPress behavior with hooks

Example: Registering theme support in `functions.php`

```
function my_theme_setup() {
    add_theme_support('title-tag');  // Auto-generates page titles
    add_theme_support('post-thumbnails');  // Enables featured images
    add_theme_support('custom-logo');  // Allows custom site logos
}
add_action('after_setup_theme', 'my_theme_setup');
```

Organizing Theme Directories

A clean and structured theme improves **maintainability and scalability**.

1. The Assets Directory (`assets/`)

The `assets/` folder stores **CSS, JavaScript, and images**.

```
assets/
├── css/      → Stylesheets (e.g., main.css, admin.css)
├── js/       → JavaScript files (e.g., main.js, custom.js)
├── images/   → Theme images (e.g., logos, icons)
```

Example: Enqueueing styles and scripts in `functions.php`

```
function my_theme_enqueue_scripts() {
   wp_enqueue_style('main-style', get_template_directory_uri() . '/assets/css/main.css', [],
'1.0');
   wp_enqueue_script('custom-js', get_template_directory_uri() . '/assets/js/custom.js',
['jquery'], '1.0', true);
}
add_action('wp_enqueue_scripts', 'my_theme_enqueue_scripts');
```

2. The Template Parts Directory (`template-parts/`)

Stores reusable components like **post loops, navigation, and hero sections**.

```
template-parts/
├── header/
│   ├── header-main.php
│   ├── header-alt.php
```

```
├── footer/
│   ├── footer-main.php
│   ├── footer-alt.php
├── post/
│   ├── content.php
│   ├── content-single.php
```

Example: Including template parts in a theme file

```
get_template_part('template-parts/post/content', 'single');
```

This loads `template-parts/post/content-single.php`.

---

3. The Includes Directory (`inc/`)

Stores **modular PHP files** for better code organization.

```
inc/
├── custom-post-types.php
├── theme-customizer.php
├── shortcodes.php
```

Instead of writing everything in `functions.php`, we **include** additional files:

```
require get_template_directory() . '/inc/custom-post-types.php';
require get_template_directory() . '/inc/theme-customizer.php';
```

---

4. The Languages Directory (`languages/`)

For **internationalization and localization**, store translation files in this directory.

```
languages/
├── my-custom-theme.pot
├── my-custom-theme-fr_FR.mo
├── my-custom-theme-es_ES.po
```

To enable theme translations:

```
function my_theme_load_textdomain() {
    load_theme_textdomain('my-custom-theme', get_template_directory() . '/languages');
}
add_action('after_setup_theme', 'my_theme_load_textdomain');
```

Best Practices for Theme File Naming and Organization

1. **Use descriptive names** – `page-about.php`, `header-main.php`, `content-single.php`.
2. **Follow WordPress standards** – Use lowercase with hyphens (`custom-post-types.php` not `customPostTypes.php`).
3. **Keep code modular** – Split large functions into separate files in `/inc/`.
4. **Use `get_template_part()`** for reusability instead of duplicating code.

5. **Avoid hardcoding URLs** – Use `get_template_directory_uri()` instead.

Summary

A well-structured theme is critical for **scalability, maintainability, and WordPress compatibility**.

✔ **Core theme files** include `style.css`, `functions.php`, and `index.php`.
✔ Organize themes with **directories like assets/, template-parts/, and inc/**.
✔ Use **naming conventions** that follow WordPress standards.
✔ Keep **functions modular** by placing them in `inc/` and including them in `functions.php`.
✔ Use **WordPress functions (`get_template_part()`, `wp_enqueue_style()`)** for efficiency.

By following these principles, your themes will be **professional, scalable, and easy to maintain**.

Creating Custom Page Templates

Custom page templates allow you to design **unique layouts for specific pages** in a WordPress theme. Instead of using the default page.php template for all pages, you can create **customized templates** to control the look and feel of different sections of your site, such as **landing pages, about pages, portfolio pages, and contact pages**.

In this chapter, you will learn:

- The **purpose of custom page templates**
- How to **create and assign custom page templates**
- How to **use conditional logic** for flexible layouts
- Best practices for **organizing and optimizing templates**

By the end of this chapter, you will be able to build fully custom page templates **without unnecessary duplication** while keeping your theme **organized and scalable**.

Understanding Custom Page Templates

WordPress uses **template files** to display different types of content. The default template for pages is page.php, but sometimes, you need **a different layout for specific pages**—this is where **custom page templates** come in.

Why Use Custom Page Templates?

✔ Design **unique layouts** for individual pages (e.g., Home, Contact, Services).
✔ Create **full-width layouts** without sidebars.
✔ Use **specialized templates** for landing pages or sales pages.
✔ Reduce **theme complexity** by avoiding excessive conditionals in page.php.

Creating a Custom Page Template

To create a custom page template, follow these steps:

1. Create a New Template File

In your theme folder (/wp-content/themes/your-theme/), create a new file:

/wp-content/themes/my-theme/page-custom.php

2. Add Template Header Comment

WordPress recognizes custom page templates by a **special comment** at the top of the file.

```php
<?php
/*
Template Name: Custom Page
*/
get_header(); ?>

<main class="custom-page">
```

```
    <h1><?php the_title(); ?></h1>
    <div class="content">
        <?php the_content(); ?>
    </div>
</main>

<?php get_footer(); ?>
```

3. Assign the Template in WordPress

1. Go to **Pages > Add New** or edit an existing page.
2. In the **Page Attributes** section (right sidebar), locate the **Template** dropdown.
3. Select **Custom Page** and update the page.

Now, when you view this page, WordPress will use `page-custom.php` instead of `page.php`.

Building a Full-Width Page Template

A **full-width page template** is useful when you want to remove the sidebar and use the entire screen width.

Example: Full-Width Page Template (`page-fullwidth.php`)

```php
<?php
/*
Template Name: Full-Width Page
*/
get_header(); ?>

<main class="fullwidth-container">
    <h1><?php the_title(); ?></h1>
    <div class="fullwidth-content">
        <?php the_content(); ?>
    </div>
</main>

<?php get_footer(); ?>
```

Add CSS for Styling (`style.css`)

```css
.fullwidth-container {
    max-width: 1200px;
    margin: 0 auto;
    padding: 20px;
}

.fullwidth-content {
    width: 100%;
}
```

This creates a **full-width page layout** that **removes sidebars** while keeping a centered content area.

Using Conditional Logic in Templates

You can create **dynamic templates** by using **conditional logic** inside your custom page templates.

Example: Display Content Based on User Role

```php
<?php
/*
Template Name: Member-Only Page
*/
get_header(); ?>

<main class="member-area">
    <h1><?php the_title(); ?></h1>
    <?php if (is_user_logged_in()) : ?>
        <p>Welcome, <?php echo wp_get_current_user()->display_name; ?>!</p>
        <?php the_content(); ?>
    <?php else : ?>
        <p>You must be logged in to view this content.</p>
        <a href="<?php echo wp_login_url(); ?>">Login Here</a>
    <?php endif; ?>
</main>

<?php get_footer(); ?>
```

This template **hides content from non-logged-in users** and prompts them to log in.

Creating a Custom Query Inside a Page Template

You can use `WP_Query` to display custom content inside a page template.

Example: Displaying Latest Blog Posts

```php
<?php
/*
Template Name: Blog Posts Page
*/
get_header(); ?>

<main class="blog-posts">
    <h1>Latest Posts</h1>
    <?php
    $args = array(
        'post_type'      => 'post',
        'posts_per_page' => 5
    );
    $custom_query = new WP_Query($args);

    if ($custom_query->have_posts()) :
        while ($custom_query->have_posts()) : $custom_query->the_post(); ?>
            <h2><a href="<?php the_permalink(); ?>"><?php the_title(); ?></a></h2>
            <p><?php the_excerpt(); ?></p>
        <?php endwhile;
        wp_reset_postdata();
    else :
```

```
        echo '<p>No posts found.</p>';
    endif;
    ?>
</main>

<?php get_footer(); ?>
```

This dynamically **fetches and displays the latest blog posts** when the template is used.

Best Practices for Custom Page Templates

✔ **Use meaningful names** (`page-landing.php`, `page-portfolio.php`).
✔ **Keep templates DRY (Don't Repeat Yourself)** by reusing `get_template_part()`.
✔ **Use the Customizer** to allow users to modify template content.
✔ **Minimize conditionals in templates** to improve performance.
✔ **Use template parts** (`get_template_part()`) to avoid excessive duplication.

Summary

Custom page templates provide a **powerful way to create unique layouts** without modifying core theme files.

✔ **Custom templates override the default page.php** and allow for unique designs.
✔ **They can be assigned per-page** using the WordPress admin.
✔ **Full-width templates** remove the sidebar for better design flexibility.
✔ **Conditional logic** can be used to modify templates dynamically.
✔ **Custom queries (WP_Query)** allow fetching specific data for templates.

By leveraging **custom page templates**, you can build **highly flexible, professional WordPress themes** that meet specific project needs.

Dynamic Content with Template Parts

A well-structured WordPress theme relies on **template parts** to create **reusable, modular** components. Instead of duplicating code across multiple templates, **template parts** allow developers to build dynamic, maintainable themes that are easier to manage and extend.

In this chapter, you will learn:

- What **template parts** are and why they are essential
- How to use **get_template_part()** for reusability
- Creating **modular templates** for headers, footers, sidebars, and custom layouts
- Using **dynamic content in template parts**
- Best practices for structuring **reusable components**

By the end of this chapter, you will be able to build **efficient WordPress themes** using **dynamic template parts** that improve maintainability and performance.

What Are Template Parts?

Template parts are modular sections of a WordPress theme that can be **included inside other templates**. They prevent code duplication and make it easier to update specific parts of a theme.

Common examples of **template parts** include:

✔ **Header (`header.php`)** – Shared across all pages
✔ **Footer (`footer.php`)** – Consistent across the site
✔ **Sidebar (`sidebar.php`)** – Used in pages with widgets
✔ **Post content (`content.php`)** – Displays blog post excerpts
✔ **Navigation (`menu.php`)** – Custom menus and navigation

Instead of repeating the same code in `index.php`, `single.php`, and `page.php`, you can **extract reusable sections into template parts**.

Using `get_template_part()` for Reusability

The `get_template_part()` function loads reusable template files dynamically.

Basic Usage

```
get_template_part('template-parts/content', 'single');
```

This will load:

/template-parts/content-single.php

If the file **does not exist**, WordPress **ignores** the call without breaking the site.

Creating Modular Template Parts

1. Creating a Custom Header Template

Instead of hardcoding your header.php, create **multiple header versions**.

1. Create a folder inside your theme:

   /template-parts/header/

2. Create a custom header file:

   /template-parts/header/header-main.php

3. Add custom HTML and PHP:

```php
<!DOCTYPE html>
<html <?php language_attributes(); ?>>
<head>
    <meta charset="<?php bloginfo('charset'); ?>">
    <meta name="viewport" content="width=device-width, initial-scale=1">
    <?php wp_head(); ?>
</head>
<body <?php body_class(); ?>>

<header class="main-header">
    <h1><?php bloginfo('name'); ?></h1>
    <nav><?php wp_nav_menu(['theme_location' => 'primary']); ?></nav>
</header>
```

4. Load the header dynamically in header.php:

```php
get_template_part('template-parts/header/header', 'main');
```

This approach allows **different headers for different sections** (e.g., header-home.php, header-minimal.php).

---

2. Creating a Custom Post Loop Template

To display blog posts dynamically, use a **post loop template part**.

1. Create a folder:

   /template-parts/post/

2. Create content.php inside the folder:

```php
<article id="post-<?php the_ID(); ?>" <?php post_class(); ?>>
    <h2><a href="<?php the_permalink(); ?>"><?php the_title(); ?></a></h2>
    <p><?php the_excerpt(); ?></p>
</article>
```

3. Include it in index.php and archive.php:

```php
if (have_posts()) :
    while (have_posts()) : the_post();
        get_template_part('template-parts/post/content');
```

```
    endwhile;
endif;
```

Now, you **reuse the same loop** across your theme.

---

3. Creating a Sidebar Template

Sidebars often contain **widgets, menus, and additional content**. Instead of hardcoding them in multiple templates, create a **sidebar template part**.

1. Create `sidebar.php`:

```
<aside class="sidebar">
    <?php dynamic_sidebar('main-sidebar'); ?>
</aside>
```

2. Include it in `page.php` and `single.php`:

```
if (is_active_sidebar('main-sidebar')) {
    get_sidebar();
}
```

This method ensures your **sidebar remains consistent** across pages.

Using Dynamic Data in Template Parts

Template parts **support dynamic content** using **WordPress functions and variables**.

Example 1: Dynamic Featured Image in Post Content

Modify `content.php` to **display the post thumbnail dynamically**:

```
<article>
    <?php if (has_post_thumbnail()) : ?>
        <div class="post-thumbnail">
            <a href="<?php the_permalink(); ?>">
                <?php the_post_thumbnail('medium'); ?>
            </a>
        </div>
    <?php endif; ?>

    <h2><a href="<?php the_permalink(); ?>"><?php the_title(); ?></a></h2>
    <p><?php the_excerpt(); ?></p>
</article>
```

Now, every post that has a **featured image** will display it automatically.

Example 2: Passing Variables to Template Parts

You can **pass data dynamically** when including template parts using `set_query_var()`.

1. In `index.php`, set a variable:

```
set_query_var('custom_message', 'Welcome to My Blog!');
get_template_part('template-parts/post/content', 'home');
```

2. In `content-home.php`, retrieve the variable:

```php
<?php
$message = get_query_var('custom_message');
if ($message) {
    echo "<p>$message</p>";
}
?>
```

This method is useful when you need **custom variations of the same template part**.

Best Practices for Using Template Parts

✔ **Organize template parts into folders** (`/template-parts/header/`, `/template-parts/post/`).
✔ **Use `get_template_part()` instead of `include()`** for compatibility.
✔ **Pass dynamic data using `set_query_var()`** to create flexible templates.
✔ **Use conditionals (`if (is_single())`) to load different versions** of template parts.
✔ **Keep template parts modular** to ensure maintainability.

Summary

Using **template parts** makes themes more **organized, scalable, and easier to manage**.

✔ **Reduce code duplication** by storing reusable components in `/template-parts/`.
✔ **Use `get_template_part()`** to load headers, footers, sidebars, and content dynamically.
✔ **Pass data to template parts** with `set_query_var()`.
✔ **Use modular structure** (`header-main.php`, `content-single.php`) for flexibility.
✔ **Improve maintainability** by keeping functions and template logic **separate**.

By mastering **template parts**, you can build **efficient and scalable WordPress themes** with **dynamic content** that adapts to different pages and sections.

Theme Customization API: Adding User Controls

The **WordPress Theme Customization API** provides developers with a structured way to create **user-friendly theme settings** that can be modified in real-time using the WordPress Customizer. Instead of requiring users to edit theme files or use third-party options panels, the Customizer offers a **native interface** to adjust theme settings with **live previews**.

In this chapter, you will learn:

- What the **Theme Customization API** is and why it's useful
- How to **register custom settings** using the Customizer
- How to create **theme options like logos, colors, and layouts**
- How to use **controls, sections, and settings** to enhance user experience
- Best practices for **keeping theme settings efficient and maintainable**

By mastering the Customization API, you can **enhance your theme's flexibility**, making it easier for users to customize without touching code.

What is the Theme Customization API?

The **Theme Customization API** allows developers to add **theme-specific options** to the WordPress Customizer (`Appearance > Customize`).

Why use the Customization API?

✔ Provides a **real-time preview** of changes before saving
✔ Keeps theme settings organized in the **WordPress Customizer**
✔ Reduces reliance on **third-party theme options panels**
✔ Stores settings in the **WordPress database (`wp_options` table)**
✔ Ensures **theme settings are portable and easily exported**

Registering Customizer Settings

To add custom settings, you must:

1. **Register a setting** – Stores the user's customization value.
2. **Add a control** – Provides a user-friendly UI (text field, dropdown, etc.).
3. **Display the setting in the theme** – Use the stored value dynamically.

Basic Example: Adding a Custom Logo Option

Add the following code to `functions.php` to **register a custom logo option**:

```php
function my_theme_customize_register($wp_customize) {
    // Add a new section
    $wp_customize->add_section('my_theme_logo_section', array(
        'title'    => __('Logo', 'my-theme'),
        'priority' => 30,
    ));

    // Add a setting
    $wp_customize->add_setting('my_theme_logo', array(
```

```
        'default'   => '',
        'transport' => 'refresh',
        'sanitize_callback' => 'esc_url_raw',
    ));

    // Add a control (file uploader)
    $wp_customize->add_control(new WP_Customize_Image_Control($wp_customize,
'my_theme_logo', array(
        'label'    => __('Upload Logo', 'my-theme'),
        'section'  => 'my_theme_logo_section',
        'settings' => 'my_theme_logo',
    )));
}

add_action('customize_register', 'my_theme_customize_register');
```

Displaying the Custom Logo in the Theme

Use the stored **theme setting** inside header.php to display the logo dynamically:

```
$custom_logo = get_theme_mod('my_theme_logo');
if ($custom_logo) {
    echo '<img src="' . esc_url($custom_logo) . '" alt="Site Logo">';
}
```

Now, users can upload and change the logo from **Appearance > Customize > Logo**.

Adding Custom Text and Color Controls

1. Creating a Custom Footer Text Setting

```
function my_theme_customize_footer($wp_customize) {
    $wp_customize->add_section('my_theme_footer_section', array(
        'title'    => __('Footer Settings', 'my-theme'),
        'priority' => 40,
    ));

    $wp_customize->add_setting('my_theme_footer_text', array(
        'default'   => 'Powered by WordPress',
        'transport' => 'refresh',
        'sanitize_callback' => 'sanitize_text_field',
    ));

    $wp_customize->add_control('my_theme_footer_text', array(
        'label'    => __('Footer Text', 'my-theme'),
        'section'  => 'my_theme_footer_section',
        'settings' => 'my_theme_footer_text',
        'type'     => 'text',
    ));
}

add_action('customize_register', 'my_theme_customize_footer');
```

Displaying the Custom Footer Text

```php
echo esc_html(get_theme_mod('my_theme_footer_text', 'Powered by WordPress'));
```

---

2. Adding a Custom Background Color Setting

```php
function my_theme_customize_colors($wp_customize) {
    $wp_customize->add_setting('my_theme_bg_color', array(
        'default'   => '#ffffff',
        'transport' => 'refresh',
        'sanitize_callback' => 'sanitize_hex_color',
    ));

    $wp_customize->add_control(new WP_Customize_Color_Control($wp_customize,
'my_theme_bg_color', array(
        'label'    => __('Background Color', 'my-theme'),
        'section'  => 'colors',
        'settings' => 'my_theme_bg_color',
    )));
}

add_action('customize_register', 'my_theme_customize_colors');
```

Applying the Background Color to CSS

```php
$bg_color = get_theme_mod('my_theme_bg_color', '#ffffff');
?>
<style>
    body {
        background-color: <?php echo esc_attr($bg_color); ?>;
    }
</style>
```

Using Select Dropdowns for Layout Options

You can provide **layout options (e.g., Sidebar Left, Sidebar Right, Full Width)** using a **select dropdown control**.

```php
function my_theme_customize_layout($wp_customize) {
    $wp_customize->add_section('my_theme_layout_section', array(
        'title'    => __('Layout Settings', 'my-theme'),
        'priority' => 50,
    ));

    $wp_customize->add_setting('my_theme_layout', array(
        'default'   => 'right-sidebar',
        'transport' => 'refresh',
        'sanitize_callback' => 'sanitize_text_field',
    ));

    $wp_customize->add_control('my_theme_layout', array(
        'label'    => __('Select Layout', 'my-theme'),
```

```
        'section'  => 'my_theme_layout_section',
        'settings' => 'my_theme_layout',
        'type'     => 'select',
        'choices'  => array(
            'left-sidebar'  => __('Left Sidebar', 'my-theme'),
            'right-sidebar' => __('Right Sidebar', 'my-theme'),
            'full-width'    => __('Full Width', 'my-theme'),
        ),
    ));
}


add_action('customize_register', 'my_theme_customize_layout');
```

Applying Layout Selection in page.php

```php
$layout = get_theme_mod('my_theme_layout', 'right-sidebar');

if ($layout == 'left-sidebar') {
    get_sidebar();
}
?>

<main class="<?php echo esc_attr($layout); ?>">
    <?php the_content(); ?>
</main>

<?php if ($layout == 'right-sidebar') {
    get_sidebar();
} ?>
```

Best Practices for Using the Theme Customization API

✔ Use `sanitize_callback` **functions** to secure user inputs.
✔ Use **default values** to prevent empty settings.
✔ **Organize settings into sections** (`add_section()`) for better UX.
✔ Use `transport => 'postMessage'` for live previews without reloading the page.
✔ **Avoid excessive settings**—only add controls that improve user experience.

Summary

The **Theme Customization API** allows users to modify theme settings **without touching code**, providing **a seamless user experience**.

✔ **Register settings** using `add_setting()` and `add_control()`.
✔ **Provide UI controls** (text, colors, images, dropdowns) in the Customizer.
✔ **Display user-defined settings dynamically** in templates.
✔ **Use the Customizer for logos, colors, layouts, and footer text.**
✔ **Follow best practices** to ensure security and maintainability.

By integrating **user-friendly theme options**, you can create **professional, customizable WordPress themes**.

Responsive Design with WordPress Themes

Responsive design is a **critical aspect of modern web development**, ensuring that websites **adapt seamlessly** across different screen sizes and devices. Since a significant portion of web traffic comes from **mobile devices**, optimizing your WordPress theme for responsiveness is **essential for usability, SEO, and user engagement**.

In this chapter, we will cover:

- The **principles of responsive design**
- Using **CSS media queries** to adjust layouts
- Implementing **flexible grids and containers**
- Using **responsive typography and images**
- Ensuring **navigation and menus** work across all screen sizes
- Testing and debugging responsive themes

By mastering these techniques, you will create **WordPress themes that look great on desktops, tablets, and mobile devices**, providing a **seamless user experience**.

Understanding Responsive Design

Responsive design ensures that a website:

✔ **Adapts fluidly** to different screen sizes (desktop, tablet, mobile).
✔ **Uses flexible layouts** instead of fixed widths.
✔ **Prioritizes mobile usability** with touch-friendly elements.
✔ **Optimizes loading speeds** by serving appropriate assets based on the device.

Key Concepts in Responsive Design

Concept	Description
Fluid Layouts	Uses percentages and flexible units (instead of fixed pixels) to define widths.
CSS Media Queries	Applies different styles based on screen size or resolution.
Responsive Images	Ensures images scale proportionally and load optimized versions for different devices.
Flexible Typography	Uses em, rem, or vw units to scale text dynamically.
Mobile-First Approach	Designs for **mobile screens first**, then scales up for larger devices.

Setting Up a Responsive WordPress Theme

1. Using a Mobile-First Approach

A **mobile-first** approach means designing for **smaller screens first** and **scaling up** for larger devices. This ensures **performance optimization** on mobile devices.

Start your **CSS styles** with **base mobile styles**, then apply **media queries** for larger screens.

Example:

```
body {
    font-size: 16px;
    line-height: 1.6;
}

/* Larger screens */
@media (min-width: 768px) {
    body {
        font-size: 18px;
    }
}

@media (min-width: 1024px) {
    body {
        font-size: 20px;
    }
}
```

---

2. Using CSS Media Queries

Media queries allow you to **apply different styles based on screen width**.

Example: Adjusting layout for different screen sizes:

```
/* Default mobile styles */
.container {
    width: 100%;
    padding: 10px;
}

/* Tablet (768px and larger) */
@media (min-width: 768px) {
    .container {
        width: 80%;
        margin: auto;
    }
}

/* Desktop (1024px and larger) */
@media (min-width: 1024px) {
    .container {
        width: 60%;
    }
}
```

Common Breakpoints:

Device Type	Min Width
Mobile	0px (default styles)

Tablet	768px
Small Desktop	1024px
Large Desktop	1280px

Implementing a Responsive Grid System

A **grid system** helps structure content dynamically. Instead of fixed widths, use **flexbox or CSS Grid** for **flexible layouts**.

1. Using CSS Flexbox for Layouts

```css
.flex-container {
    display: flex;
    flex-wrap: wrap;
    justify-content: space-between;
}

.flex-item {
    flex: 1 1 100%;
    padding: 10px;
}

/* Tablet layout */
@media (min-width: 768px) {
    .flex-item {
        flex: 1 1 45%;
    }
}

/* Desktop layout */
@media (min-width: 1024px) {
    .flex-item {
        flex: 1 1 30%;
    }
}
```

This structure allows items to **adjust dynamically** across screen sizes.

2. Using CSS Grid for Layouts

```css
.grid-container {
    display: grid;
    grid-template-columns: 1fr;
    gap: 10px;
}

/* Tablet layout */
@media (min-width: 768px) {
    .grid-container {
        grid-template-columns: 1fr 1fr;
    }
}
```

```
/* Desktop layout */
@media (min-width: 1024px) {
    .grid-container {
        grid-template-columns: 1fr 1fr 1fr;
    }
}
```

Flexbox vs. Grid:

Feature	Flexbox	CSS Grid
Best for	**Row-based layouts**	**Complex grid structures**
Alignment	**One-dimensional** (row or column)	**Two-dimensional** (row & column)
Browser Support	**Excellent**	**Good (modern browsers)**

Optimizing Responsive Typography

Typography should scale with the screen size for readability.

Use rem or vw for fluid typography:

```
body {
    font-size: 16px;
}

@media (min-width: 768px) {
    body {
        font-size: 1.1rem;
    }
}

@media (min-width: 1024px) {
    body {
        font-size: 1.2rem;
    }
}
```

Making Images Responsive

Images should **resize properly** and **load optimized versions** based on device type.

1. Using max-width for Scalable Images

```
img {
    max-width: 100%;
    height: auto;
}
```

2. Using WordPress's Responsive Image Features

WordPress **automatically generates multiple sizes** of uploaded images. Use `srcset` for optimal loading:

```html
<img src="<?php echo esc_url(get_the_post_thumbnail_url(null, 'medium')); ?>"
    srcset="<?php echo esc_url(get_the_post_thumbnail_url(null, 'large')); ?> 1024w,
            <?php echo esc_url(get_the_post_thumbnail_url(null, 'medium')); ?> 768w"
    sizes="(max-width: 768px) 100vw, 50vw"
    alt="<?php the_title_attribute(); ?>">
```

Creating a Responsive Navigation Menu

Navigation should be **touch-friendly and adaptable** for mobile users.

1. Making a Mobile Menu Toggle

```css
.nav-menu {
    display: none;
}

@media (min-width: 768px) {
    .nav-menu {
        display: block;
    }
}
```

2. Using JavaScript for a Mobile Toggle Button

```javascript
document.getElementById('menu-toggle').addEventListener('click', function() {
    document.getElementById('nav-menu').classList.toggle('open');
});
```

Add this to the theme:

```html
<button id="menu-toggle">☰ Menu</button>
<nav id="nav-menu" class="nav-menu">
    <?php wp_nav_menu(['theme_location' => 'primary']); ?>
</nav>
```

Testing and Debugging Responsive WordPress Themes

✔ **Test using Chrome DevTools** (F12 > `Toggle Device Toolbar`).
✔ **Use BrowserStack or Responsinator** for cross-device testing.
✔ **Ensure fast loading times** on mobile using **Google Lighthouse** (`Ctrl + Shift + I > Lighthouse`).
✔ **Use real devices** to check touch usability and scrolling behavior.

Summary

Responsive design ensures **WordPress themes provide an optimal user experience** across all devices.

✔ **Use a mobile-first approach** and **CSS media queries** to create fluid layouts.
✔ **Implement flexbox or CSS Grid** for adaptable page structures.
✔ **Use responsive typography and images** to improve readability and performance.
✔ **Optimize navigation menus** for mobile devices.
✔ **Test and debug across multiple devices** using Chrome DevTools and Lighthouse.

By integrating **responsive design techniques**, your WordPress themes will be **user-friendly, future-proof, and SEO-optimized**.

Optimizing Theme Performance

Performance optimization is a **critical aspect of WordPress theme development**, ensuring that your theme loads **fast, efficiently, and smoothly** across devices. A well-optimized theme improves **user experience, search engine rankings (SEO), and overall site performance**.

In this chapter, you will learn:

- How to **minimize HTTP requests** and optimize assets
- Best practices for **lazy loading images and videos**
- How to **reduce database queries and improve caching**
- Techniques to **defer and async JavaScript and CSS**
- How to **measure and test performance** with Lighthouse and other tools

By the end of this chapter, you will be able to **create high-performance WordPress themes** that are **fast, lightweight, and scalable**.

Understanding Theme Performance Bottlenecks

Before optimizing, it's important to **identify what slows down WordPress themes**.

Common Performance Issues:

Issue	Impact
Unoptimized Images	Increases page load time and bandwidth usage.
Excessive HTTP Requests	Too many CSS, JS, and font files slow down loading.
Bloated Theme Files	Large theme files add unnecessary load.
Inefficient Database Queries	Slows down page rendering.
No Caching Strategy	Pages are generated dynamically for each user instead of serving a cached version.
Blocking JavaScript & CSS	Prevents pages from loading efficiently.

Optimizing your theme addresses these issues, leading to **faster page loads** and better user experience.

Reducing HTTP Requests

Every asset loaded on a webpage (**CSS, JavaScript, fonts, images**) requires an HTTP request. Reducing the number of requests speeds up loading times.

1. Combine and Minify CSS and JavaScript

Before Optimization:
Your theme loads multiple stylesheets and JavaScript files:

```
<link rel="stylesheet" href="style.css">
```

```
<link rel="stylesheet" href="header.css">
<link rel="stylesheet" href="footer.css">
<script src="jquery.js"></script>
<script src="custom.js"></script>
```

After Optimization (Combining and Minifying):

```
<link rel="stylesheet" href="style.min.css">
<script src="scripts.min.js"></script>
```

How to Minify CSS and JavaScript:
Use online tools like **CSS Minifier** or WordPress plugins like:
✔ **Autoptimize**
✔ **WP Rocket**
✔ **Fast Velocity Minify**

Alternatively, use **Gulp or Webpack** to automate minification:

```
npm install -g terser
terser custom.js -o custom.min.js
```

Optimizing Images for Faster Loading

Images are **one of the biggest performance bottlenecks**. Use these best practices:

1. Use Proper Image Formats

- Use **JPEG** for photos, **PNG** for transparent images, and **WebP** for modern compression.
- Convert images to WebP format:

```
cwebp -q 80 image.jpg -o image.webp
```

2. Resize Images for Different Devices

Use **responsive images** to serve different sizes based on screen size:

```
<img src="image-600.jpg"
     srcset="image-300.jpg 300w, image-600.jpg 600w, image-1200.jpg 1200w"
     sizes="(max-width: 600px) 100vw, (max-width: 1200px) 50vw, 600px"
     alt="Optimized Image">
```

3. Enable Lazy Loading

Lazy loading **delays image loading** until they are needed:

```
<img src="placeholder.jpg" data-src="actual-image.jpg" class="lazyload">
```

For WordPress 5.5+ (Native Lazy Loading):

```
<img src="image.jpg" loading="lazy" alt="Lazy loaded image">
```

Leveraging Browser Caching

Browser caching **stores static assets** (CSS, JavaScript, images) locally on users' devices.

Add these rules to your **.htaccess** file:

```
<IfModule mod_expires.c>
    ExpiresActive On
    ExpiresByType text/css "access plus 1 year"
    ExpiresByType image/jpeg "access plus 1 year"
    ExpiresByType image/png "access plus 1 year"
    ExpiresByType application/javascript "access plus 1 year"
</IfModule>
```

Alternatively, use caching plugins:
✔ **WP Rocket**
✔ **W3 Total Cache**
✔ **WP Super Cache**

Defer and Async JavaScript for Faster Rendering

JavaScript **blocks page rendering** if not loaded properly. Use **async or defer** attributes:

```
<script src="custom.js" async></script>
<script src="analytics.js" defer></script>
```

Difference Between Async and Defer:

Attribute	Effect
Async	Loads JavaScript asynchronously and executes it immediately.
Defer	Loads JavaScript asynchronously but executes after HTML parsing.

Best Practice: Use async for **third-party scripts** and defer for **theme scripts**.

Reducing Database Queries

Too many database queries slow down performance. Use **efficient WordPress functions** to minimize queries.

1. Use transients for Caching Queries

Instead of querying the database every time a page loads, store the result temporarily using **transients**.

```
function get_custom_posts() {
    $cached_posts = get_transient('custom_posts');

    if (false === $cached_posts) {
        $query = new WP_Query([
            'post_type' => 'post',
            'posts_per_page' => 5
        ]);

        $cached_posts = $query->posts;
```

```
        set_transient('custom_posts', $cached_posts, HOUR_IN_SECONDS);
    }

    return $cached_posts;
}
```

Using Content Delivery Networks (CDN)

A **CDN (Content Delivery Network)** speeds up loading by **serving assets from multiple global locations**.

Popular CDNs:
✔ **Cloudflare**
✔ **KeyCDN**
✔ **BunnyCDN**

To use a CDN, modify `wp-config.php`:

```
define('WP_CONTENT_URL', 'https://cdn.example.com/wp-content');
define('WP_PLUGIN_URL', 'https://cdn.example.com/wp-content/plugins');
```

Measuring and Testing Theme Performance

Regularly test performance using these tools:

Tool	Purpose
Google Lighthouse	Measures performance, accessibility, and best practices.
GTmetrix	Analyzes page load speed and optimization recommendations.
Pingdom Tools	Monitors website performance over time.
WebPageTest	Provides advanced testing with waterfall charts.

Using Lighthouse in Chrome DevTools:

1. Open Chrome DevTools (`Ctrl + Shift + I` or `Cmd + Option + I`).
2. Go to the **Lighthouse** tab.
3. Click **Generate Report** to analyze performance.

Best Practices for Optimizing WordPress Themes

✔ **Minify and combine CSS & JS** to reduce HTTP requests.
✔ **Use optimized images** (WebP, lazy loading, responsive sizes).
✔ **Enable caching** for faster load times.
✔ **Defer and async JavaScript** to prevent render blocking.
✔ **Use transients** to cache database queries.

✔ **Implement a CDN** to serve assets globally.
✔ **Regularly test performance** using Lighthouse and GTmetrix.

Summary

A **fast, well-optimized theme** enhances **user experience, SEO rankings, and conversion rates**.

✔ **Reduce HTTP requests** by minifying and combining assets.
✔ **Optimize images and enable lazy loading** for faster page loads.
✔ **Leverage caching and CDNs** to improve performance.
✔ **Use async and defer JavaScript** to prevent render blocking.
✔ **Monitor and test performance regularly** using Lighthouse and GTmetrix.

By implementing these **performance optimization strategies**, you can ensure your **WordPress themes run efficiently**, providing **a seamless experience** for all users.

Section 4:
Developing Custom Plugins

Plugin Structure: Bootstrapping and Best Practices

Developing custom WordPress plugins requires a **solid structure, clean code, and adherence to best practices** to ensure security, maintainability, and compatibility. A well-structured plugin improves **scalability, performance, and extensibility** while avoiding conflicts with other themes and plugins.

In this chapter, we will cover:

- The **fundamental structure** of a WordPress plugin
- How to properly **bootstrap a plugin**
- Best practices for **naming conventions and file organization**
- The importance of **using hooks and WordPress APIs**
- How to ensure **security and performance** in plugin development

By the end of this chapter, you will be able to create a **modular, well-structured plugin** that adheres to **WordPress coding standards and best practices**.

Understanding the WordPress Plugin Structure

A WordPress plugin consists of **PHP scripts** that extend or modify WordPress functionality. Plugins can range from **simple tweaks** to **complex applications** with custom post types, settings pages, and external API integrations.

A **properly structured plugin** makes maintenance easier and prevents conflicts with other plugins and themes.

Setting Up a WordPress Plugin

1. Creating the Plugin Folder

All plugins are stored in:

/wp-content/plugins/

Create a new plugin folder:

/wp-content/plugins/my-custom-plugin/

2. Creating the Main Plugin File

Inside the new folder, create my-custom-plugin.php (the main entry file). This file must contain **plugin metadata** for WordPress to recognize it.

```php
<?php
/**
 * Plugin Name: My Custom Plugin
 * Plugin URI: https://example.com
 * Description: A custom WordPress plugin for demonstration purposes.
 * Version: 1.0
 * Author: Your Name
 * Author URI: https://example.com
 * License: GPL2
 * License URI: https://www.gnu.org/licenses/gpl-2.0.html
 * Text Domain: my-custom-plugin
 */
```

3. Registering the Plugin with WordPress

Navigate to **Plugins > Installed Plugins** in the WordPress admin panel, and you will see "My Custom Plugin" listed. Click **Activate** to enable it.

Best Practices for Plugin Structure

A properly structured plugin improves **code organization, reusability, and scalability**.

Recommended Plugin Structure

```
my-custom-plugin/
|── my-custom-plugin.php  (Main plugin file)
|── uninstall.php  (Clean up on uninstall)
|── includes/
|    ├── admin-settings.php  (Admin page settings)
|    ├── custom-functions.php  (Helper functions)
|── assets/
|    ├── css/
|    |    ├── admin-style.css  (Admin panel styles)
|    |    ├── public-style.css  (Frontend styles)
|    ├── js/
|    |    ├── admin-script.js  (Admin panel scripts)
|    |    ├── public-script.js  (Frontend scripts)
|── templates/
|    ├── custom-template.php  (Frontend display template)
|── languages/
|    ├── my-custom-plugin-en_US.mo  (Translation files)
```

Why use this structure?
✔ **Separation of concerns** – Admin and frontend logic are separate.
✔ **Easier maintenance** – Modular files simplify debugging.
✔ **Scalability** – Additional features can be added without disrupting existing code.

Bootstrapping a WordPress Plugin

Bootstrapping refers to the **initialization process** of a plugin, ensuring it loads efficiently and interacts with WordPress properly.

1. Using Hooks for Initialization

Instead of running code directly, **use WordPress hooks** to ensure your plugin loads at the right time.

```
function my_custom_plugin_init() {
    // Register custom post types, scripts, or other setup tasks
}
add_action('plugins_loaded', 'my_custom_plugin_init');
```

Why use plugins_loaded?
✔ Ensures that all plugins are **fully loaded** before executing plugin code.
✔ Prevents **function conflicts** between plugins.

Enqueuing Scripts and Styles

To ensure styles and scripts **load properly and do not conflict** with other plugins, use wp_enqueue_scripts().

1. Enqueue Frontend CSS and JavaScript

```
function my_custom_plugin_enqueue_scripts() {
    wp_enqueue_style('my-plugin-style', plugin_dir_url(__FILE__) .
'assets/css/public-style.css', [], '1.0');
    wp_enqueue_script('my-plugin-script', plugin_dir_url(__FILE__) .
'assets/js/public-script.js', ['jquery'], '1.0', true);
}
add_action('wp_enqueue_scripts', 'my_custom_plugin_enqueue_scripts');
```

2. Enqueue Admin Panel Styles and Scripts

```
function my_custom_plugin_admin_scripts() {
    wp_enqueue_style('my-plugin-admin-style', plugin_dir_url(__FILE__) .
'assets/css/admin-style.css', [], '1.0');
    wp_enqueue_script('my-plugin-admin-script', plugin_dir_url(__FILE__) .
'assets/js/admin-script.js', ['jquery'], '1.0', true);
}
add_action('admin_enqueue_scripts', 'my_custom_plugin_admin_scripts');
```

Using Hooks and Filters in Plugins

Hooks allow **interaction with WordPress core functions** without modifying core files.

1. Using Action Hooks

Execute custom code **at specific points** in WordPress execution.

Example: Adding content **before post content**

```
function my_plugin_add_before_content($content) {
    if (is_single()) {
        return '<p>Custom message before content</p>' . $content;
    }
    return $content;
}
```

```
add_action('the_content', 'my_plugin_add_before_content');
```

2. Using Filter Hooks

Modify **existing content or functionality** dynamically.

Example: Adding a **custom class to post titles**

```
function my_plugin_custom_title_class($title) {
    return '<span class="custom-title">' . $title . '</span>';
}
add_filter('the_title', 'my_plugin_custom_title_class');
```

Securing Your Plugin

1. Prevent Direct File Access

Ensure users cannot **directly access plugin files** by adding:

```
if (!defined('ABSPATH')) {
    exit; // Exit if accessed directly
}
```

2. Use Nonces for Form Security

When processing forms in WordPress, **use nonces to prevent CSRF attacks**.

```
function my_plugin_display_form() {
    ?>
    <form method="post">
        <?php wp_nonce_field('my_plugin_form_action', 'my_plugin_nonce'); ?>
        <input type="text" name="user_input">
        <input type="submit" value="Submit">
    </form>
    <?php
}

function my_plugin_handle_form_submission() {
    if (isset($_POST['my_plugin_nonce']) &&
wp_verify_nonce($_POST['my_plugin_nonce'], 'my_plugin_form_action')) {
        // Process the form data
    } else {
        die('Security check failed!');
    }
}
add_action('init', 'my_plugin_handle_form_submission');
```

Best Practices for Plugin Development

✔ **Use WordPress hooks** (`add_action`, `add_filter`) instead of modifying core files.
✔ **Follow WordPress coding standards** to maintain compatibility.
✔ **Keep code modular** – Separate functionality into different files.
✔ **Use nonces** to secure forms and prevent CSRF attacks.

✔ **Escape user input** using `esc_html()`, `esc_attr()`, and `sanitize_text_field()`.
✔ **Follow proper naming conventions** to prevent conflicts (`my_plugin_function_name`).
✔ **Document your code** to make it readable and maintainable.

Summary

A **well-structured WordPress plugin** ensures **efficiency, security, and maintainability**.

✔ **Follow a modular plugin structure** for easier development.
✔ **Bootstrap using hooks (`plugins_loaded`)** to initialize safely.
✔ **Enqueue scripts and styles properly** to avoid conflicts.
✔ **Use WordPress action and filter hooks** for flexibility.
✔ **Implement security measures** like **nonces and escaping user input**.

By following these **best practices**, you can develop **scalable, secure, and professional WordPress plugins**.

Hooks 101: Actions, Filters, and Priority

Hooks are the foundation of WordPress extensibility, allowing themes and plugins to interact with **WordPress core functionality** without modifying core files. Understanding **actions, filters, and priority** is essential for building custom plugins, modifying themes, and ensuring compatibility with other WordPress components.

In this chapter, we will cover:

- What **actions** and **filters** are and how they differ
- How to use hooks to **extend WordPress functionality**
- How **hook priority** affects execution order
- Practical examples of **using hooks in plugins and themes**
- Best practices for **working with WordPress hooks efficiently**

By mastering hooks, you will be able to **modify WordPress behavior dynamically**, making your themes and plugins **more flexible and scalable**.

Understanding Hooks in WordPress

WordPress hooks allow developers to **inject custom code** at specific points in execution. Hooks are divided into two main types:

Hook Type	Purpose
Action Hooks	Execute code at specific points in WordPress (e.g., adding content, loading scripts).
Filter Hooks	Modify or filter existing data before it's displayed (e.g., modifying post titles, excerpts).

Both action and filter hooks **use the add_action() and add_filter() functions** to attach custom functions.

Action Hooks: Executing Code at Specific Events

Actions allow you to run custom code **when specific events occur** in WordPress.

Basic Syntax of Action Hooks

```
add_action('hook_name', 'custom_function', \$priority, \$accepted_args);
```

Parameter	Description
`hook_name`	The name of the WordPress hook.
`custom_function`	The function that runs when the hook is triggered.
`\$priority`	(Optional) Determines the execution order of the function (default is 10).

\$accepted_args	(Optional) The number of arguments the function accepts (default is 1).

Example 1: Adding Custom Content Before Posts

```
function my_custom_message_before_post($content) {
    if (is_single()) {
        $message = '<p style="color: red; font-weight: bold;">Warning: This is
a custom message before the content.</p>';
        return $message . $content;
    }
    return $content;
}
add_action('the_content', 'my_custom_message_before_post');
```

What This Does:

✔ Adds a **custom message before post content** dynamically.

✔ Applies only to **single post pages** (is_single()).

Example 2: Adding a Custom Footer Message

```
function my_custom_footer_message() {
    echo '<p style="text-align: center;">© 2024 My Custom Plugin. All rights
reserved.</p>';
}
add_action('wp_footer', 'my_custom_footer_message');
```

What This Does:

✔ Adds a **custom message to the footer** of every page.

✔ Uses wp_footer (executed before the </body> tag).

Example 3: Enqueueing Styles and Scripts Using Actions

The **correct way to load CSS and JavaScript** in WordPress is by using wp_enqueue_scripts.

```
function my_plugin_enqueue_styles() {
    wp_enqueue_style('my-plugin-style', plugin_dir_url(__FILE__) .
'assets/css/style.css', [], '1.0');
    wp_enqueue_script('my-plugin-script', plugin_dir_url(__FILE__) .
'assets/js/script.js', ['jquery'], '1.0', true);
}
add_action('wp_enqueue_scripts', 'my_plugin_enqueue_styles');
```

✔ Ensures scripts are loaded **only when needed**.

✔ Avoids **conflicts with other plugins and themes**.

Filter Hooks: Modifying Data Before Display

Filters modify or format data before it is displayed or processed. Unlike actions, **filters must return a value**.

Basic Syntax of Filter Hooks

```
add_filter('hook_name', 'custom_function', \$priority, \$accepted_args);
```

Parameter	Description
hook_name	The name of the WordPress filter hook.
custom_function	The function that processes and modifies data.
\$priority	(Optional) Determines execution order (default is 10).
\$accepted_args	(Optional) Number of arguments the function accepts (default is 1).

Example 1: Modifying the Post Title

```
function my_custom_post_title($title) {
    return '[Custom] ' . $title;
}
add_filter('the_title', 'my_custom_post_title');
```

✔ Adds a [Custom] prefix to **all post titles** dynamically.

Example 2: Modifying the Excerpt Length

```
function my_custom_excerpt_length($length) {
    return 20; // Sets excerpt length to 20 words
}
add_filter('excerpt_length', 'my_custom_excerpt_length');
```

✔ Shortens all post excerpts to **20 words**.

Example 3: Changing Login Logo URL

Modify the WordPress login page logo **to link to a custom site**:

```
function my_custom_login_url($url) {
    return home_url(); // Redirects to site homepage
}
add_filter('login_headerurl', 'my_custom_login_url');
```

✔ When users click the login page logo, they are redirected to **the homepage** instead of WordPress.org.

Understanding Hook Priority

Hook priority controls the execution order of multiple functions attached to the same hook.

✔ **Lower numbers execute first** (e.g., add_action('init', 'my_function', 5) runs before add_action('init', 'other_function', 10)).

Example: Controlling Execution Order

```
function first_function() {
    echo 'First Function Executed<br>';
}
add_action('wp_footer', 'first_function', 5);

function second_function() {
    echo 'Second Function Executed<br>';
}
add_action('wp_footer', 'second_function', 10);
```

✔ first_function() runs **before** second_function() because it has a **lower priority (5 vs. 10)**.

Removing Hooks

You can **remove** actions and filters if necessary.

Removing an Action Hook

```
remove_action('wp_footer', 'my_custom_footer_message');
```

✔ Prevents my_custom_footer_message() from executing in wp_footer.

Removing a Filter Hook

```
remove_filter('the_title', 'my_custom_post_title');
```

✔ Prevents my_custom_post_title() from modifying post titles.

Best Practices for Using Hooks

✔ **Always use meaningful function names** to avoid conflicts (my_plugin_add_footer_message()).
✔ **Use lower priority values for critical functions** (e.g., database queries).
✔ **Use remove_action() and remove_filter() when needed** to avoid duplicate behavior.
✔ **Check for function existence** before adding actions to prevent errors:

```
if (!function_exists('my_plugin_custom_function')) {
    function my_plugin_custom_function() {
        // Function logic
    }
}
```

✔ **Keep filters performant** – Avoid **heavy database queries** inside filter hooks.

Summary

Hooks are **one of the most powerful features of WordPress**, allowing developers to extend and modify WordPress functionality **without modifying core files**.

✔ **Actions execute functions** at specific points (`add_action()`).
✔ **Filters modify and return data** before it's displayed (`add_filter()`).
✔ **Priority controls execution order** (lower numbers run first).
✔ **Hooks improve code flexibility, reusability, and maintainability**.
✔ **Remove hooks when necessary** using `remove_action()` and `remove_filter()`.

By mastering **actions, filters, and priority**, you can build **efficient, extendable, and conflict-free plugins**.

Creating Custom Post Types and Taxonomies

WordPress comes with default post types like **posts, pages, attachments, revisions, and navigation menus**, but often, websites require **custom content structures** beyond these. This is where **Custom Post Types (CPTs) and Custom Taxonomies** come into play.

By defining **custom post types**, developers can create structured content such as **portfolios, events, products, testimonials, or team members**. Custom taxonomies allow **categorization beyond default WordPress categories and tags**, enabling a better content organization system.

In this chapter, we will cover:

- **What are Custom Post Types and Taxonomies?**
- How to **register custom post types (CPTs) programmatically**
- Creating **custom taxonomies** for advanced content classification
- Displaying custom post types in themes
- Best practices for managing CPTs and taxonomies efficiently

By the end of this chapter, you will be able to **create and manage structured content types** in WordPress **like a professional**.

Understanding Custom Post Types

A **Custom Post Type (CPT)** is a user-defined content type in WordPress. It functions **like default posts and pages**, but is tailored to store **specific types of content**.

Examples of Custom Post Types:

✔ **Portfolio** – Showcasing past projects
✔ **Testimonials** – Collecting customer reviews
✔ **Events** – Managing upcoming events
✔ **Products** – Custom post type for eCommerce
✔ **Real Estate Listings** – Managing property listings

Registering a Custom Post Type

To create a **custom post type**, use the `register_post_type()` function inside a plugin or theme's `functions.php` file.

Example: Creating a Custom Post Type for "Portfolio"

```php
function my_custom_post_type() {
    $args = array(
        'labels'            => array(
            'name'          => __('Portfolios', 'text-domain'),
            'singular_name' => __('Portfolio', 'text-domain'),
        ),
        'public'            => true,
        'menu_icon'         => 'dashicons-portfolio',
        'has_archive'       => true,
        'supports'          => array('title', 'editor', 'thumbnail', 'excerpt'),
        'rewrite'           => array('slug' => 'portfolio'),
        'show_in_rest'      => true, // Enables Gutenberg support
```

```
    );

    register_post_type('portfolio', $args);
}
add_action('init', 'my_custom_post_type');
```

✔ Creates a **new menu item "Portfolio"** in the admin panel.
✔ Enables **title, editor, featured image, and excerpt** support.
✔ Adds a **custom URL structure (example.com/portfolio/)**.
✔ Enables **REST API support** for headless WordPress projects.

Displaying Custom Post Types in Themes

Once a CPT is registered, it needs to be **displayed on the frontend**.

1. Creating a Custom Archive Template

WordPress automatically looks for an `archive-{post-type}.php` template for CPTs.

To display **all portfolio items**, create:

/wp-content/themes/your-theme/archive-portfolio.php

Inside `archive-portfolio.php`:

```php
<?php get_header(); ?>

<h1>Our Portfolio</h1>

<?php if (have_posts()) : while (have_posts()) : the_post(); ?>
    <article>
        <h2><a href="<?php the_permalink(); ?>"><?php the_title(); ?></a></h2>
        <p><?php the_excerpt(); ?></p>
    </article>
<?php endwhile; endif; ?>

<?php get_footer(); ?>
```

✔ Displays a **list of portfolio items** dynamically.

---

2. Creating a Custom Single Template

To display a **single portfolio entry**, create:

/wp-content/themes/your-theme/single-portfolio.php

Inside `single-portfolio.php`:

```php
<?php get_header(); ?>

<article>
    <h1><?php the_title(); ?></h1>
```

```php
    <?php if (has_post_thumbnail()) { the_post_thumbnail('large'); } ?>
    <div><?php the_content(); ?></div>
</article>

<?php get_footer(); ?>
```

✔ Displays **portfolio content dynamically** using `the_title()`, `the_post_thumbnail()`, and `the_content()`.

Creating Custom Taxonomies

A **taxonomy** is a way to group similar content. WordPress has **default taxonomies**:

- **Categories** (hierarchical)
- **Tags** (non-hierarchical)

Custom taxonomies allow you to **categorize custom post types more effectively**.

Example: Registering a "Project Type" Taxonomy for Portfolio

```php
function my_custom_taxonomy() {
    $args = array(
        'labels'            => array(
            'name'          => __('Project Types', 'text-domain'),
            'singular_name' => __('Project Type', 'text-domain'),
        ),
        'public'            => true,
        'hierarchical'      => true, // Works like categories
        'show_in_rest'      => true, // Enables Gutenberg support
        'rewrite'           => array('slug' => 'project-type'),
    );

    register_taxonomy('project_type', 'portfolio', $args);
}
add_action('init', 'my_custom_taxonomy');
```

✔ Creates a **hierarchical** taxonomy for Portfolio (like Categories).
✔ Registers a **URL structure (example.com/project-type/design)**.

Displaying Custom Taxonomies

Once a taxonomy is registered, you can display it in **single portfolio pages**.

1. Displaying Taxonomies in a Post Loop

Inside `archive-portfolio.php` or `single-portfolio.php`, add:

```php
<?php
$terms = get_the_terms(get_the_ID(), 'project_type');
if ($terms && !is_wp_error($terms)) {
    echo '<ul>';
    foreach ($terms as $term) {
```

```
       echo '<li><a href="' . get_term_link($term) . '">' . $term->name .
'</a></li>';
    }
    echo '</ul>';
}
?>
```

✔ Displays **assigned "Project Types"** for each portfolio item.

Querying Custom Post Types

To display **custom post types on any page**, use `WP_Query()`.

Example: Fetching Portfolio Items

```
$args = array(
    'post_type'      => 'portfolio',
    'posts_per_page' => 5,
    'order'          => 'DESC',
);
$query = new WP_Query($args);

if ($query->have_posts()) : while ($query->have_posts()) : $query->the_post();
    echo '<h2><a href="' . get_permalink() . '">' . get_the_title() . '</a></h2>';
endwhile; endif;

wp_reset_postdata();
```

✔ Fetches **latest 5 portfolio items**.

Best Practices for Custom Post Types and Taxonomies

✔ **Use `init` hook** to register CPTs and taxonomies properly.
✔ **Use `show_in_rest => true`** for Gutenberg and REST API compatibility.
✔ **Keep CPT and taxonomy names lowercase and hyphenated** (e.g., `portfolio`, `project-type`).
✔ **Always create archive and single templates** for better theme integration.
✔ **Use `flush_rewrite_rules()` when adding new CPTs** to refresh permalinks.

Summary

Custom post types and taxonomies **extend WordPress functionality**, making it a powerful CMS for **structured content**.

✔ **CPTs store specialized content** (e.g., Portfolio, Events, Products).
✔ **Custom taxonomies organize content** beyond default categories/tags.
✔ **Use `register_post_type()` and `register_taxonomy()`** for custom structures.
✔ **Create archive and single templates** for displaying CPTs properly.
✔ **Use WP_Query()** to fetch custom content dynamically.

By following **best practices**, you can **build structured, scalable WordPress websites** tailored to different industries.

Adding Admin Menus and Settings Pages

Custom **admin menus and settings pages** allow plugin and theme developers to provide **a user-friendly interface for configuring settings**. Instead of relying on hardcoded options, users can modify plugin behavior **directly from the WordPress admin panel**.

In this chapter, you will learn:

- How to **add custom admin menus** in WordPress
- How to create **submenus and settings pages**
- How to **save and retrieve plugin settings** using the WordPress **Settings API**
- Best practices for organizing admin settings efficiently

By the end of this chapter, you will be able to create **fully functional admin panels** for WordPress plugins and themes.

Adding a Custom Admin Menu

Basic Syntax of `add_menu_page()`

To add a custom menu in the **WordPress Admin Panel**, use add_menu_page().

```
add_menu_page(
    $page_title,
    $menu_title,
    $capability,
    $menu_slug,
    $function,
    $icon_url,
    $position
);
```

Parameter	Description
\$page_title	Title of the settings page.
\$menu_title	Label shown in the WordPress dashboard.
\$capability	User role required to access the menu.
\$menu_slug	Unique slug for the menu.
\$function	Callback function that outputs the menu page content.
\$icon_url	Icon displayed in the admin menu.
\$position	Position in the WordPress menu hierarchy.

Example: Creating a Custom Admin Menu for a Plugin

```
function my_plugin_create_menu() {
```

```
    add_menu_page(
        'My Plugin Settings',        // Page Title
        'My Plugin',                 // Menu Title
        'manage_options',            // Capability (Admin only)
        'my-plugin-settings',        // Menu Slug
        'my_plugin_settings_page',   // Callback Function
        'dashicons-admin-generic',   // Icon
        90                           // Position
    );
}
add_action('admin_menu', 'my_plugin_create_menu');
```

Creating the Callback Function

The my_plugin_settings_page() function renders the menu page content.

```
function my_plugin_settings_page() {
    ?>
    <div class="wrap">
        <h1>My Plugin Settings</h1>
        <p>Welcome to the settings page for My Plugin.</p>
    </div>
    <?php
}
```

✔ This **adds a menu item** in the WordPress admin panel.
✔ Clicking it opens a page titled **"My Plugin Settings"**.

Adding Submenus to the Custom Menu

Submenus allow **multiple settings pages** under a main menu. Use add_submenu_page().

Example: Creating Submenus Under "My Plugin"

```
function my_plugin_create_submenus() {
    add_submenu_page(
        'my-plugin-settings',    // Parent Menu Slug
        'General Settings',      // Page Title
        'General',               // Submenu Title
        'manage_options',        // Capability
        'my-plugin-general',     // Submenu Slug
        'my_plugin_general_settings_page' // Callback Function
    );

    add_submenu_page(
        'my-plugin-settings',
        'Advanced Settings',
        'Advanced',
        'manage_options',
        'my-plugin-advanced',
        'my_plugin_advanced_settings_page'
    );
}
```

```
add_action('admin_menu', 'my_plugin_create_submenus');
```

✔ This adds **"General" and "Advanced" submenus** under the **"My Plugin" menu**.

Creating a Settings Page with Form Fields

To store and retrieve settings, use the **WordPress Settings API**.

1. Registering Settings

```
function my_plugin_register_settings() {
    register_setting('my_plugin_options_group', 'my_plugin_option');
}
add_action('admin_init', 'my_plugin_register_settings');
```

✔ Registers a **setting named my_plugin_option** in the WordPress database.

---

2. Creating a Settings Form

Modify my_plugin_settings_page() to include a settings form.

```
function my_plugin_settings_page() {
    ?>
    <div class="wrap">
        <h1>My Plugin Settings</h1>
        <form method="post" action="options.php">
            <?php
            settings_fields('my_plugin_options_group'); // Security fields
            do_settings_sections('my_plugin_settings'); // Output settings sections
            submit_button();
            ?>
        </form>
    </div>
    <?php
}
```

✔ This generates a **fully functional WordPress settings form**.

---

3. Adding a Text Input Field

To display a **text input field** for users to configure settings:

```
function my_plugin_settings_fields() {
    add_settings_section(
        'my_plugin_main_section',    // Section ID
        'Main Settings',             // Section Title
        null,                        // Callback (optional)
        'my_plugin_settings'         // Page Slug
    );

    add_settings_field(
        'my_plugin_option_field',    // Field ID
        'Custom Text',               // Field Label
```

```
        'my_plugin_option_callback', // Callback Function
        'my_plugin_settings',        // Page Slug
        'my_plugin_main_section'      // Section ID
    );
}
add_action('admin_init', 'my_plugin_settings_fields');

function my_plugin_option_callback() {
    $value = get_option('my_plugin_option', '');
    echo '<input type="text" name="my_plugin_option" value="' .
esc_attr($value) . '">';
}
```

✔ This adds a **custom text input field** under **"My Plugin Settings"**.

Retrieving Saved Plugin Settings

Retrieve the saved settings anywhere in WordPress using:

```
$custom_option = get_option('my_plugin_option');
echo 'Custom Option: ' . esc_html($custom_option);
```

✔ Fetches the stored value from the database dynamically.

Best Practices for Admin Menus and Settings

✔ **Use meaningful slugs** (my-plugin-settings, my-plugin-general).
✔ **Ensure security** – Only admins (manage_options) should access settings.
✔ **Use the WordPress Settings API** instead of storing raw data in the database.
✔ **Escape user input** using esc_attr() and esc_html().
✔ **Use transients for performance** when loading frequently accessed options.

Summary

Adding **custom admin menus and settings pages** makes **WordPress plugins more user-friendly**.

✔ **Use add_menu_page()** to create custom admin menus.
✔ **Use add_submenu_page()** to add submenus.
✔ **Use the Settings API (register_setting())** to store settings properly.
✔ **Use get_option()** to retrieve user-defined settings dynamically.
✔ **Follow best security practices** to prevent unauthorized access.

By implementing these techniques, you can **create professional, well-structured settings pages** for your WordPress plugins.

Handling Form Submissions Securely

Forms are a fundamental part of WordPress plugins, allowing users to submit **contact requests, login credentials, settings updates, and custom data**. However, improperly handling form submissions can lead to **security vulnerabilities**, including **Cross-Site Request Forgery (CSRF), Cross-Site Scripting (XSS), and SQL Injection**.

In this chapter, you will learn:

- How to create and **handle form submissions properly**
- How to **sanitize and validate user input**
- How to implement **WordPress nonces for CSRF protection**
- Best practices for **securely processing form data**

By the end of this chapter, you will be able to **build secure and efficient WordPress forms** that prevent attacks and ensure data integrity.

Creating a Secure Form in WordPress

To secure a WordPress form, follow these **three key steps**:

✔ **Sanitize and validate user input** before storing it.
✔ **Use WordPress nonces** to protect against CSRF attacks.
✔ **Ensure safe database interactions** using prepared statements.

Step 1: Creating a Basic Form with Nonces

Let's create a **simple contact form** inside a WordPress plugin.

```php
function my_custom_form() {
    ?>
    <form method="post" action="">
        <?php wp_nonce_field('my_form_action', 'my_form_nonce'); ?>
        <label for="user_name">Name:</label>
        <input type="text" name="user_name" required>

        <label for="user_email">Email:</label>
        <input type="email" name="user_email" required>

        <label for="user_message">Message:</label>
        <textarea name="user_message" required></textarea>

        <input type="submit" name="submit_form" value="Submit">
    </form>
    <?php
}
add_shortcode('my_custom_form', 'my_custom_form');
```

✔ This form **generates a WordPress nonce (`wp_nonce_field()`)**, which prevents CSRF attacks.
✔ It uses **the `add_shortcode()` function**, so you can insert `[my_custom_form]` into any post or page.

Step 2: Handling the Form Submission

Now, we need a function to **process and validate** the form data.

```php
function my_custom_form_handler() {
    if (isset($_POST['submit_form'])) {

        // Verify the nonce for CSRF protection
        if (!isset($_POST['my_form_nonce']) ||
!wp_verify_nonce($_POST['my_form_nonce'], 'my_form_action')) {
            wp_die('Security check failed. Please try again.');
        }

        // Sanitize input data
        $name = sanitize_text_field($_POST['user_name']);
        $email = sanitize_email($_POST['user_email']);
        $message = sanitize_textarea_field($_POST['user_message']);

        // Validate email format
        if (!is_email($email)) {
            wp_die('Invalid email address.');
        }

        // Process the form data (e.g., store in database, send email)
        wp_mail('admin@example.com', 'New Contact Form Submission', "Name:
$name\nEmail: $email\nMessage: $message");

        // Redirect after submission
        wp_redirect(home_url('/thank-you'));
        exit;
    }
}
add_action('init', 'my_custom_form_handler');
```

✔ **Verifies the nonce** (`wp_verify_nonce()`) to prevent CSRF attacks.
✔ **Sanitizes and validates user input** using WordPress functions.
✔ **Uses `wp_mail()`** to send an email notification.
✔ **Redirects users** after submission to avoid duplicate form submissions.

Sanitizing and Validating User Input

WordPress provides built-in **sanitization and validation functions** to prevent malicious input.

Sanitization Functions

Function	Purpose
`sanitize_text_field(\$input)`	Removes HTML and unwanted characters.
`sanitize_email(\$input)`	Validates and sanitizes an email address.
`sanitize_textarea_field(\$input)`	Strips HTML tags from text areas.

sanitize_url(\$input)	Ensures the URL format is correct.
esc_html(\$input)	Escapes HTML to prevent XSS attacks.

Validation Functions

Function	Purpose
is_email(\$email)	Checks if an email address is valid.
filter_var(\$input, FILTER_VALIDATE_URL)	Validates URLs.
preg_match()	Custom pattern matching for advanced validation.

Example: Validating a Phone Number

```
$phone = $_POST['user_phone'];
if (!preg_match('/^\+?[0-9\s\-]+$/', $phone)) {
    wp_die('Invalid phone number format.');
}
```

✔ Ensures the **phone number** contains only digits, spaces, +, or -.

Storing Form Data Securely in the Database

When saving form data in the database, always use **prepared statements** to prevent SQL injection.

Example: Storing Form Data in a Custom Table

```
global $wpdb;
$wpdb->insert(
    $wpdb->prefix . 'custom_forms',
    array(
        'name'    => $name,
        'email'   => $email,
        'message' => $message
    ),
    array('%s', '%s', '%s') // Data formats: string, string, string
);
```

✔ Uses **$wpdb->insert()** instead of raw SQL queries.
✔ **Prevents SQL injection** by defining data types (%s for strings).

Securing File Uploads in Forms

If your form allows file uploads (e.g., profile pictures, resumes), **follow strict security rules**.

Example: Handling Secure File Uploads

```
if (!empty($_FILES['upload_file']['name'])) {
```

```
    $allowed_types = array('image/jpeg', 'image/png', 'application/pdf');

    if (!in_array($_FILES['upload_file']['type'], $allowed_types)) {
        wp_die('Invalid file type.');
    }

    $upload = wp_upload_bits($_FILES['upload_file']['name'], null,
file_get_contents($_FILES['upload_file']['tmp_name']));

    if ($upload['error']) {
        wp_die('File upload failed.');
    }

    $file_url = $upload['url']; // Save file URL
}
```

✔ **Restricts file types** to prevent malicious uploads.
✔ Uses `wp_upload_bits()` instead of direct file system access.

Preventing Spam with Google reCAPTCHA

To prevent **spam form submissions**, integrate Google **reCAPTCHA v3**.

Step 1: Register reCAPTCHA

Get API keys from **[Google reCAPTCHA]** (https://www.google.com/recaptcha/intro/).

Step 2: Add reCAPTCHA to the Form

```
<script
src="https://www.google.com/recaptcha/api.js?render=your_site_key"></script>
<script>
grecaptcha.ready(function() {
    grecaptcha.execute('your_site_key', {action: 'submit'}).then(function(token) {
        document.getElementById('g-recaptcha-response').value = token;
    });
});
</script>

<input type="hidden" name="g-recaptcha-response" id="g-recaptcha-response">
```

Step 3: Verify reCAPTCHA in PHP

```
$recaptcha_secret = 'your_secret_key';
$response = $_POST['g-recaptcha-response'];
$verify =
wp_remote_get("https://www.google.com/recaptcha/api/siteverify?secret=$recaptc
ha_secret&response=$response");

$verify_data = json_decode(wp_remote_retrieve_body($verify));
if (!$verify_data->success) {
    wp_die('reCAPTCHA verification failed.');
}
```

✔ Prevents **automated bot submissions** effectively.

Best Practices for Secure Form Handling

✔ **Always use nonces** (`wp_nonce_field()`, `wp_verify_nonce()`) to prevent CSRF.
✔ **Sanitize and validate user input** before storing it.
✔ **Use `\$wpdb->insert()`** to prevent SQL injection.
✔ **Restrict file uploads** to safe types (JPEG, PNG, PDF).
✔ **Implement reCAPTCHA** to prevent spam bots.
✔ **Redirect after form submission** to avoid duplicate submissions.

Summary

Handling form submissions **securely** is crucial for preventing **security vulnerabilities** in WordPress.

✔ **Use nonces** to protect against CSRF attacks.
✔ **Sanitize and validate input** to prevent XSS and SQL injection.
✔ **Use `\$wpdb->insert()`** instead of raw queries.
✔ **Secure file uploads** with MIME type restrictions.
✔ **Implement Google reCAPTCHA** to block spam.

By following **these security best practices**, you can ensure **safe, reliable, and professional** WordPress form handling.

Integrating AJAX in Plugins

AJAX (Asynchronous JavaScript and XML) enables WordPress plugins to perform **dynamic updates** without requiring a full page reload. This is essential for **interactive features** like live search, contact forms, voting systems, and real-time updates.

In this chapter, you will learn:

- How AJAX works in WordPress.
- How to enqueue scripts and handle AJAX requests.
- Securing AJAX requests with nonces.
- Using AJAX for **frontend and backend processing**.
- Best practices for **efficient AJAX implementation**.

By the end of this chapter, you will be able to **integrate AJAX into your plugins** for improved user experience and performance.

Understanding AJAX in WordPress

AJAX allows **asynchronous communication** between the browser and the server, meaning users can interact with your plugin without **reloading the page**.

WordPress AJAX Flow:

1. **User action** triggers an AJAX request (e.g., clicking a button).
2. **JavaScript sends a request** to admin-ajax.php in WordPress.
3. **WordPress processes the request** via a registered PHP function.
4. **Response is returned to JavaScript** for real-time updates.

Enqueuing JavaScript for AJAX

AJAX requires **JavaScript for sending requests** and **PHP for processing them**.

Step 1: Load JavaScript in Your Plugin

First, enqueue a JavaScript file (ajax-script.js) in your plugin.

```
function my_plugin_enqueue_ajax_script() {
    wp_enqueue_script('my-ajax-script', plugin_dir_url(__FILE__) .
'js/ajax-script.js', array('jquery'), null, true);

    wp_localize_script('my-ajax-script', 'my_ajax_object', array(
        'ajax_url' => admin_url('admin-ajax.php'), // AJAX endpoint
        'nonce'    => wp_create_nonce('my_ajax_nonce') // Security nonce
    ));
}
add_action('wp_enqueue_scripts', 'my_plugin_enqueue_ajax_script');
```

✔ wp_localize_script() passes PHP data (AJAX URL, nonce) to JavaScript.

Handling AJAX Requests in JavaScript

Create a js/ajax-script.js file inside your plugin:

```javascript
jQuery(document).ready(function($) {
    $('#my-button').on('click', function(e) {
        e.preventDefault();

        $.ajax({
            type: 'POST',
            url: my_ajax_object.ajax_url,
            data: {
                action: 'my_ajax_action',
                security: my_ajax_object.nonce,
                message: 'Hello, AJAX!'
            },
            success: function(response) {
                $('#response-container').html(response);
            },
            error: function() {
                alert('AJAX request failed!');
            }
        });
    });
});
```

✔ This sends a POST request to admin-ajax.php.
✔ The action 'my_ajax_action' is used to process the request.
✔ security sends the nonce for security verification.

Handling AJAX Requests in PHP

Now, handle the AJAX request in functions.php or your plugin file.

```php
function my_plugin_handle_ajax_request() {
    // Verify nonce for security
    check_ajax_referer('my_ajax_nonce', 'security');

    // Get data from request
    $message = isset($_POST['message']) ?
sanitize_text_field($_POST['message']) : '';

    // Process the request (e.g., database update, API call)
    $response = 'Server Response: ' . esc_html($message);

    // Send response
    echo $response;
    wp_die(); // Always end AJAX functions with wp_die()
}
add_action('wp_ajax_my_ajax_action', 'my_plugin_handle_ajax_request');
add_action('wp_ajax_nopriv_my_ajax_action', 'my_plugin_handle_ajax_request');
// Allows non-logged-in users
```

✔ `check_ajax_referer()` **validates the nonce** for security.

✔ `\$_POST['message']` retrieves data sent via AJAX.

✔ `wp_ajax_my_ajax_action` processes requests for logged-in users.

✔ `wp_ajax_nopriv_my_ajax_action` allows **non-logged-in users** to access the AJAX action.

Implementing AJAX for a Live Search Feature

A **real-time search** feature improves user experience by showing results dynamically as users type.

1. Create the Search Input Field

Add this inside a page or template:

```
<input type="text" id="search-input" placeholder="Search...">
<div id="search-results"></div>
```

---

2. JavaScript: Send Search Query via AJAX

Modify `ajax-script.js` to listen for input changes:

```
jQuery(document).ready(function($) {
    $('#search-input').on('keyup', function() {
        let query = $(this).val();

        if (query.length < 2) {
            $('#search-results').html('');
            return;
        }

        $.ajax({
            type: 'POST',
            url: my_ajax_object.ajax_url,
            data: {
                action: 'live_search',
                security: my_ajax_object.nonce,
                query: query
            },
            success: function(response) {
                $('#search-results').html(response);
            }
        });
    });
});
```

---

3. PHP: Process Search Query and Return Results

Handle the request inside your plugin:

```
function my_plugin_live_search() {
    check_ajax_referer('my_ajax_nonce', 'security');
```

```php
    $query = isset($_POST['query']) ? sanitize_text_field($_POST['query']) :
'';

    $args = array(
        'post_type'      => 'post',
        'posts_per_page' => 5,
        's'              => $query
    );

    $search_query = new WP_Query($args);

    if ($search_query->have_posts()) {
        while ($search_query->have_posts()) {
            $search_query->the_post();
            echo '<p><a href="' . get_permalink() . '">' . get_the_title() .
'</a></p>';
        }
    } else {
        echo '<p>No results found.</p>';
    }

    wp_die();
}
add_action('wp_ajax_live_search', 'my_plugin_live_search');
add_action('wp_ajax_nopriv_live_search', 'my_plugin_live_search');
```

✔ Uses `WP_Query()` to **search for posts matching the query**.
✔ Returns search results **instantly as the user types**.

Securing AJAX Requests

✔ **Always validate nonces** using `check_ajax_referer()`.
✔ **Sanitize all input** using `sanitize_text_field()` and `esc_html()`.
✔ **Use `wp_die()`** to end AJAX requests properly.
✔ **Avoid exposing sensitive data** in AJAX responses.
✔ **Restrict access to logged-in users** when necessary (e.g., admin tasks).

Best Practices for AJAX in WordPress

✔ **Use `admin-ajax.php` only when needed** – For performance, consider using the **WordPress REST API** for complex AJAX tasks.
✔ **Minimize unnecessary AJAX calls** – Optimize scripts to prevent excessive requests.
✔ **Load AJAX scripts only where needed** – Use conditional enqueuing:

```php
if (is_page('search')) {
    wp_enqueue_script('my-ajax-script');
}
```

✔ **Use caching strategies** – For frequently accessed AJAX data, consider using **transients**:

```php
$data = get_transient('cached_ajax_response');
```

```
if (!$data) {
    // Generate response
    $data = expensive_database_query();
    set_transient('cached_ajax_response', $data, HOUR_IN_SECONDS);
}
echo $data;
```

Summary

AJAX allows **seamless, real-time interactions** in WordPress plugins without page reloads.

✔ **Use `admin-ajax.php`** as the AJAX endpoint.
✔ **Enqueue scripts properly** with `wp_localize_script()`.
✔ **Handle AJAX requests securely** with `check_ajax_referer()`.
✔ **Use AJAX for live search, voting, and dynamic content updates**.
✔ **Optimize AJAX requests** to prevent performance issues.

By integrating AJAX into your WordPress plugins, you can **enhance user experience** and **build modern, interactive applications**.

Securing Plugins: Nonces and Data Validation

Security is a **critical aspect of WordPress plugin development**. Improper handling of data can lead to **Cross-Site Request Forgery (CSRF), SQL Injection, and Cross-Site Scripting (XSS) vulnerabilities**.

To protect against these threats, WordPress provides built-in security measures like **nonces, data validation, and sanitization functions**.

In this chapter, you will learn:

- What **nonces** are and how to use them to prevent CSRF attacks.
- How to **sanitize and validate user input** before processing.
- How to **escape output data** to prevent XSS attacks.
- Best practices for **handling user input securely** in WordPress plugins.

By the end of this chapter, you will be able to **build secure WordPress plugins** that protect user data and prevent security vulnerabilities.

Understanding Nonces in WordPress

A **nonce (Number used ONCE)** is a security token that **prevents unauthorized form submissions and AJAX requests**.

WordPress nonces:
✔ Prevent **CSRF attacks**.
✔ Expire after a set time (default: 24 hours).
✔ Are unique per user and action.

Creating and Verifying a Nonce in Forms

Step 1: Add a Nonce to a Form

When creating a form inside a plugin, add a nonce for security:

```
<form method="post" action="">
    <?php wp_nonce_field('my_form_action', 'my_form_nonce'); ?>

    <label for="user_input">Enter Data:</label>
    <input type="text" name="user_input">

    <input type="submit" name="submit_form" value="Submit">
</form>
```

✔ `wp_nonce_field('action_name', 'nonce_name')` generates a hidden input field containing the nonce.
✔ This nonce must be **verified** before processing the form submission.

Step 2: Verifying the Nonce in PHP

In the form handling function, verify the nonce:

```
function my_plugin_process_form() {
    if (isset($_POST['submit_form'])) {
```

```
        // Verify nonce for CSRF protection
        if (!isset($_POST['my_form_nonce']) ||
!wp_verify_nonce($_POST['my_form_nonce'], 'my_form_action')) {
            wp_die('Security check failed.');
        }

        // Sanitize and process data
        $user_input = sanitize_text_field($_POST['user_input']);
        echo 'User Input: ' . esc_html($user_input);
    }
}
add_action('init', 'my_plugin_process_form');
```

✔ wp_verify_nonce() checks the nonce's validity.

✔ wp_die() **stops execution if the nonce check fails**.

✔ sanitize_text_field() ensures **clean input** before processing.

Using Nonces in AJAX Requests

For AJAX security, pass and verify a nonce:

Step 1: Pass the Nonce to JavaScript

```
function my_plugin_enqueue_ajax_script() {
    wp_enqueue_script('my-ajax-script', plugin_dir_url(__FILE__) .
'js/ajax-script.js', array('jquery'), null, true);

    wp_localize_script('my-ajax-script', 'my_ajax_object', array(
        'ajax_url' => admin_url('admin-ajax.php'),
        'nonce'    => wp_create_nonce('my_ajax_nonce')
    ));
}
add_action('wp_enqueue_scripts', 'my_plugin_enqueue_ajax_script');
```

✔ wp_localize_script() sends the **AJAX URL and nonce** to JavaScript.

Step 2: Send the Nonce in AJAX Request

Inside ajax-script.js:

```
jQuery(document).ready(function($) {
    $('#my-button').on('click', function() {
        $.ajax({
            type: 'POST',
            url: my_ajax_object.ajax_url,
            data: {
                action: 'my_secure_ajax_action',
                security: my_ajax_object.nonce
            },
            success: function(response) {
                alert(response);
            }
```

```
            });
        });
});
```

✔ Sends the **nonce (my_ajax_object.nonce)** along with the AJAX request.

Step 3: Verify the Nonce in PHP

```php
function my_plugin_secure_ajax() {
    // Verify nonce
    check_ajax_referer('my_ajax_nonce', 'security');

    // Process data
    echo 'Secure AJAX request processed!';
    wp_die();
}
add_action('wp_ajax_my_secure_ajax_action', 'my_plugin_secure_ajax');
add_action('wp_ajax_nopriv_my_secure_ajax_action', 'my_plugin_secure_ajax');
```

✔ `check_ajax_referer('my_ajax_nonce', 'security')` **verifies the nonce** before processing.
✔ Prevents **unauthorized AJAX requests** from external sources.

Sanitizing and Validating User Input

Sanitization **removes unwanted characters** from user input.
Validation **ensures input meets expected criteria** (e.g., email format).

Sanitizing Input Data

Function	Purpose
sanitize_text_field(\$input)	Removes HTML and unwanted characters.
sanitize_email(\$email)	Ensures email format is correct.
sanitize_textarea_field(\$input)	Strips tags from textareas.
sanitize_url(\$url)	Removes invalid URL characters.

Example:

```php
$name  = sanitize_text_field($_POST['name']);
$email = sanitize_email($_POST['email']);
$url   = sanitize_url($_POST['website']);
```

Validating Input Data

Function	Purpose
is_email(\$email)	Validates email format.

`filter_var(\$url, FILTER_VALIDATE_URL)`	Checks if a URL is valid.
`preg_match('/regex/', \$input)`	Custom validation patterns.

Example:

```
if (!is_email($email)) {
    wp_die('Invalid email address.');
}

if (!preg_match('/^[a-zA-Z0-9]+$/', $username)) {
    wp_die('Username contains invalid characters.');
}
```

✔ Prevents **malicious data injection**.

Escaping Output to Prevent XSS

Escaping ensures **safe display of user-generated content** in HTML.

Escape Functions

Function	Purpose
`esc_html(\$input)`	Escapes HTML to prevent XSS.
`esc_attr(\$input)`	Escapes attributes inside <input> tags.
`esc_url(\$input)`	Ensures safe URLs.

Example:

```
echo '<p>' . esc_html($user_message) . '</p>';
echo '<input type="text" value="' . esc_attr($user_input) . '">';
echo '<a href="' . esc_url($user_link) . '">Visit</a>';
```

✔ Prevents **malicious JavaScript from executing in the browser**.

Best Practices for Secure Plugin Development

✔ **Always use nonces** (`wp_nonce_field()`, `wp_verify_nonce()`) for forms and AJAX.
✔ **Sanitize all input** before storing (`sanitize_text_field()`, `sanitize_email()`).
✔ **Validate data** (`is_email()`, `FILTER_VALIDATE_URL`).
✔ **Escape output properly** (`esc_html()`, `esc_attr()`).
✔ **Use prepared statements** when querying the database (`\$wpdb->prepare()`).

Example: Secure database query:

```
global $wpdb;
$wpdb->prepare(
    "SELECT * FROM {$wpdb->prefix}users WHERE email = %s",
```

```
    $email
);
```

✔ Prevents **SQL injection attacks**.

Summary

Security should be **a top priority** in WordPress plugin development.

✔ **Nonces prevent CSRF attacks** (wp_nonce_field(), wp_verify_nonce()).
✔ **Sanitize input** before saving (sanitize_text_field(), sanitize_email()).
✔ **Validate data** to ensure correctness (is_email(), FILTER_VALIDATE_URL).
✔ **Escape output** to prevent XSS (esc_html(), esc_attr()).
✔ **Use secure database queries** with \$wpdb->prepare().

By following **these best practices**, you can develop **secure, professional, and reliable WordPress plugins**.

Section 5:
Advanced Theme and Plugin Techniques

Combining Themes and Plugins for Modular Design

Themes and plugins serve different roles in WordPress:

- **Themes** control the **appearance and layout** of a website.
- **Plugins** extend **functionality and features** independent of the theme.

However, **integrating themes and plugins effectively** allows for a **modular design** that improves **scalability, maintainability, and reusability**.

In this chapter, you will learn:

- How to **separate functionality from theme design** using plugins.
- How to create **theme-specific plugins** for custom functionality.
- Best practices for **communicating between themes and plugins**.
- How to use **theme support features** and **custom hooks** to improve integration.

By the end of this chapter, you will be able to **develop modular WordPress solutions** where themes and plugins work seamlessly together without dependencies.

Why Separate Functionality from Design?

Many beginners **embed functionality inside themes**, which leads to **problems when switching themes**.

Problems with Functionality in Themes

✗ **Losing Features on Theme Change** – Custom post types, shortcodes, and settings **should persist** even if a theme is changed.

✗ **Difficult Maintenance** – When code for theme styling and business logic is mixed, debugging and updates become harder.

✗ **Security Issues** – Placing PHP functions inside `functions.php` without proper validation can lead to security vulnerabilities.

■ **Solution**: Move **functionality-related code** to a **custom plugin** instead of embedding it in `functions.php`.

Creating a Theme-Specific Plugin

A **theme-specific plugin** contains functionalities **related to a theme** but **independent of its design**.

Example: Moving Custom Post Types from Theme to Plugin

Instead of registering a **Portfolio** custom post type inside `functions.php`, create a plugin:

1. Create a Plugin Folder

/wp-content/plugins/my-theme-functions/

2. Create the Plugin File

Inside /my-theme-functions/, create my-theme-functions.php:

```php
<?php
/**
 * Plugin Name: My Theme Functions
 * Description: Adds custom post types and features for MyTheme.
 * Version: 1.0
 * Author: Your Name
 */

if (!defined('ABSPATH')) {
    exit; // Prevent direct file access
}

// Register Portfolio Post Type
function my_theme_register_portfolio() {
    $args = array(
        'labels'        => array(
            'name'          => __('Portfolio', 'mytheme'),
            'singular_name' => __('Portfolio Item', 'mytheme'),
        ),
        'public'        => true,
        'has_archive'   => true,
        'supports'      => array('title', 'editor', 'thumbnail'),
        'rewrite'       => array('slug' => 'portfolio'),
    );

    register_post_type('portfolio', $args);
}
add_action('init', 'my_theme_register_portfolio');
```

✔ This **keeps the portfolio post type active** even if the theme changes.

Using `add_theme_support()` for Modular Features

Themes can declare **support for specific features** using add_theme_support().

Example: Enabling Theme Support for a Feature

Inside `functions.php`:

```php
function mytheme_add_theme_features() {
    add_theme_support('custom-logo');
    add_theme_support('post-thumbnails');
}
```

```
add_action('after_setup_theme', 'mytheme_add_theme_features');
```

✔ Ensures the theme **supports a custom logo and featured images**.

Communicating Between Themes and Plugins

Themes and plugins can **exchange data** through:

1. **Hooks and Filters** (Best practice)
2. **Theme-Specific Functions**

---

1. Using Hooks for Communication

Hooks allow **plugins to add or modify theme features** dynamically.

Example: Adding Custom Content via Hooks

Inside the theme (`functions.php`):

```
function mytheme_after_post_content($content) {
    if (is_single()) {
        $content .= apply_filters('mytheme_custom_after_content', '');
    }
    return $content;
}
add_filter('the_content', 'mytheme_after_post_content');
```

Inside the plugin:

```
function my_plugin_add_after_content($content) {
    return '<p>Extra content added by plugin.</p>';
}
add_filter('mytheme_custom_after_content', 'my_plugin_add_after_content');
```

✔ The **plugin can modify the theme's behavior** without modifying the theme files.

---

2. Using Theme-Specific Functions in Plugins

A plugin can check if a **specific theme is active** before adding features.

Example: Checking for an Active Theme

```
function my_plugin_init() {
    if (wp_get_theme() == 'MyTheme') {
        // Add MyTheme-specific features
    }
}
add_action('init', 'my_plugin_init');
```

✔ Ensures **plugin features are applied only when the correct theme is active**.

Creating a Modular Design with Child Themes

Instead of modifying a **parent theme**, use a **child theme** to extend functionality.

Example: Creating a Child Theme

1. Create a folder inside `/wp-content/themes/`:

   /wp-content/themes/mytheme-child/

2. Inside `style.css`, add:

```
/*
Theme Name: MyTheme Child
Template: mytheme
*/
```

3. Add a `functions.php` file with **extra functionality**:

```
function my_child_theme_enqueue_styles() {
    wp_enqueue_style('parent-style', get_template_directory_uri() . '/style.css');
}
add_action('wp_enqueue_scripts', 'my_child_theme_enqueue_styles');
```

✔ This **inherits all styles from the parent theme** but allows custom modifications.

Best Practices for Modular Theme and Plugin Development

✔ **Keep themes focused on design** (CSS, templates, layout).
✔ **Move functionality into a plugin** (CPTs, shortcodes, settings).
✔ **Use hooks (`add_action()`, `add_filter()`)** for theme-plugin communication.
✔ **Use `add_theme_support()`** to enable/disable theme features dynamically.
✔ **Check the active theme before running plugin-specific code**.

Summary

Combining themes and plugins in a **modular way** ensures **scalability, maintainability, and flexibility**.

✔ **Themes handle styling and presentation** (templates, layouts).
✔ **Plugins handle functionality** (custom post types, settings).
✔ **Use hooks and filters** to allow plugins to extend themes dynamically.
✔ **Use `add_theme_support()`** to register modular features.
✔ **Use child themes** to modify theme behavior safely.

By following these best practices, you can **build WordPress solutions that work efficiently across multiple themes and environments**.

Custom Gutenberg Blocks with React

The **Gutenberg editor** (also known as the **Block Editor**) introduced in WordPress 5.0 revolutionized content creation by replacing the **classic editor** with a **modern, block-based experience**. Instead of using shortcodes or custom meta fields, developers can now create **custom blocks** with **React and JavaScript**, giving users an intuitive, dynamic editing experience.

In this chapter, you will learn:

- The **structure of a Gutenberg block**
- How to **set up a development environment** for block creation
- How to create **custom static and dynamic blocks**
- How to **use React for interactive features** in Gutenberg
- Best practices for **registering and managing blocks efficiently**

By the end of this chapter, you will be able to **build and integrate custom Gutenberg blocks** into your WordPress themes and plugins.

Understanding Gutenberg Blocks

Each Gutenberg block is a **self-contained unit of content** (e.g., paragraph, image, button). Custom blocks allow developers to:

✔ Create **interactive UI elements** without shortcodes.
✔ Enhance **editor usability** with **live previews**.
✔ Improve **content structure and reusability**.

Setting Up a Gutenberg Block Development Environment

To create a Gutenberg block, you need:

- **Node.js** (for package management and JavaScript bundling)
- **WordPress Scripts** (official build tools)

1. Install Node.js

Download and install **[Node.js]** (https://nodejs.org/) (LTS version).

Verify the installation:

```
node -v
npm -v
```

2. Create a Plugin for Custom Blocks

Inside `/wp-content/plugins/`, create a folder:

/wp-content/plugins/my-custom-blocks/

Inside this folder, create `my-custom-blocks.php`:

```
<?php
/**
```

```
 * Plugin Name: My Custom Blocks
 * Description: A plugin to add custom Gutenberg blocks.
 * Version: 1.0
 * Author: Your Name
 */

if (!defined('ABSPATH')) {
    exit; // Prevent direct access
}

// Load block assets
function my_custom_blocks_enqueue() {
    wp_enqueue_script(
        'my-custom-blocks-js',
        plugin_dir_url(__FILE__) . 'build/index.js',
        array('wp-blocks', 'wp-editor', 'wp-components', 'wp-i18n', 'wp-element'),
        filemtime(plugin_dir_path(__FILE__) . 'build/index.js')
    );
}
add_action('enqueue_block_editor_assets', 'my_custom_blocks_enqueue');
```

✔ This plugin will load **our custom Gutenberg blocks** inside the WordPress editor.

Creating a Basic Gutenberg Block

1. Initialize the Block Development Environment

Inside /wp-content/plugins/my-custom-blocks/, run:

npx @wordpress/create-block my-custom-block

✔ This command **generates a block starter template** inside /my-custom-block/.

---

2. Understanding the Block Structure

The generated folder structure:

```
my-custom-block/
|── src/
|    |── edit.js        # Block editor interface
|    |── save.js        # Frontend block output
|    |── index.js       # Block registration
|── block.json          # Block metadata
|── package.json        # Dependencies
|── build/              # Compiled files (generated)
```

---

3. Registering a Basic Block

Edit src/index.js to define the block:

```
import { registerBlockType } from '@wordpress/blocks';
import { __ } from '@wordpress/i18n';
import edit from './edit';
```

```
import save from './save';

registerBlockType('my-plugin/my-custom-block', {
    title: __('Custom Block', 'my-plugin'),
    icon: 'smiley',
    category: 'common',
    edit,
    save,
});
```

✔ This **registers the block** in the Gutenberg editor.

---

4. Editing the Block (`edit.js`)

Modify `src/edit.js` to control the **editor appearance**:

```
import { __ } from '@wordpress/i18n';
import { useBlockProps } from '@wordpress/block-editor';

export default function Edit({ attributes, setAttributes }) {
    return (
        <div {...useBlockProps()}>
            <h3>{__('Hello, Gutenberg!', 'my-plugin')}</h3>
            <p>{__('Edit this text inside the block.', 'my-plugin')}</p>
        </div>
    );
}
```

✔ Displays **static text** inside the block editor.

---

5. Defining Block Output (`save.js`)

Modify `src/save.js` to define **how the block appears on the frontend**:

```
import { useBlockProps } from '@wordpress/block-editor';

export default function Save() {
    return (
        <div {...useBlockProps.save()}>
            <h3>Hello, Gutenberg!</h3>
            <p>This is a saved block.</p>
        </div>
    );
}
```

✔ Controls **what gets saved to the database** when the post is published.

---

6. Building and Activating the Block

Run the following command to **compile the block**:

```
npm run build
```

Now **activate the plugin** in **WordPress > Plugins**.

Your **custom Gutenberg block** is now available in the WordPress editor! 🎉

Creating an Interactive Block with Attributes

Blocks can **store user input** using attributes.

Example: Editable Text Block

Modify `src/index.js` to define an attribute:

```
registerBlockType('my-plugin/editable-block', {
    title: __('Editable Block', 'my-plugin'),
    icon: 'edit',
    category: 'common',
    attributes: {
        content: { type: 'string', default: 'Type something...' }
    },
    edit({ attributes, setAttributes }) {
        return (
            <input
                type="text"
                value={attributes.content}
                onChange={(e) => setAttributes({ content: e.target.value })}
            />
        );
    },
    save({ attributes }) {
        return <p>{attributes.content}</p>;
    }
});
```

✔ The user **can edit text inside the block**, and it will be **saved in the post content**.

Best Practices for Custom Gutenberg Blocks

✔ Use `block.json` **for block metadata** to simplify block registration.
✔ **Use attributes for dynamic content** (text inputs, images, styles).
✔ **Keep editor and frontend styles separate** for better customization.
✔ **Follow accessibility best practices** to ensure usability.
✔ **Use `@wordpress/scripts`** for automatic build processes (`npm run build`).

Summary

Gutenberg blocks allow developers to **extend the WordPress editor with custom, interactive features**.

✔ **Set up a development environment** with Node.js and `@wordpress/scripts`.
✔ **Register blocks** using `registerBlockType()`.

✔ Define block behavior in `edit.js` and `save.js`.
✔ Use attributes to store dynamic user input.
✔ Compile and activate the block inside a plugin.

By following **these steps and best practices**, you can **enhance the Gutenberg editor with custom React-powered blocks**, providing a seamless and modern editing experience.

Extending the WordPress Dashboard

The **WordPress Dashboard** is the **central hub** where site administrators manage content, settings, and plugins. Customizing the dashboard can **improve usability, enhance workflows, and add new functionality** tailored to specific needs.

In this chapter, you will learn:

- How to **add custom dashboard widgets**
- How to **modify the WordPress admin menu and toolbar**
- How to create **custom admin pages**
- How to customize the **login page and user experience**
- Best practices for **extending the dashboard without cluttering it**

By the end of this chapter, you will be able to **extend the WordPress admin area professionally**, improving the user experience for administrators and clients.

Adding Custom Dashboard Widgets

WordPress allows developers to **add custom widgets** to the admin dashboard using the `wp_dashboard_setup` hook.

Example: Creating a Simple Dashboard Widget

```
function my_custom_dashboard_widget() {
    wp_add_dashboard_widget(
        'custom_widget_id',
        'Custom Dashboard Widget',
        'my_custom_dashboard_content'
    );
}

function my_custom_dashboard_content() {
    echo "<p>Welcome to your custom dashboard! Here's some important info.</p>";
}

add_action('wp_dashboard_setup', 'my_custom_dashboard_widget');
```

✔ Adds a **new widget** to the **Dashboard Home page**.
✔ Displays **custom content** (HTML, text, or dynamic data).

Example: Displaying Recent Posts in a Widget

```
function my_recent_posts_dashboard_widget() {
    wp_add_dashboard_widget(
        'recent_posts_widget',
        'Recent Posts',
        'my_recent_posts_widget_content'
    );
}

function my_recent_posts_widget_content() {
    $query = new WP_Query(array('post_type' => 'post', 'posts_per_page' => 5));
```

```
    if ($query->have_posts()) {
        echo '<ul>';
        while ($query->have_posts()) {
            $query->the_post();
            echo '<li><a href="' . get_edit_post_link() . '">' . get_the_title() .
'</a></li>';
        }
        echo '</ul>';
    } else {
        echo '<p>No recent posts available.</p>';
    }
    wp_reset_postdata();
}

add_action('wp_dashboard_setup', 'my_recent_posts_dashboard_widget');
```

✔ **Displays the 5 most recent posts** as clickable links.

Customizing the Admin Menu

Adding a Custom Menu to the Admin Panel

You can create a **custom admin menu page** to **display settings, reports, or custom content**.

```
function my_custom_admin_menu() {
    add_menu_page(
        'Custom Admin Page',
        'Custom Menu',
        'manage_options',
        'custom-admin-page',
        'my_custom_admin_page_content',
        'dashicons-admin-generic',
        90
    );
}

function my_custom_admin_page_content() {
    echo "<h1>Welcome to My Custom Admin Page</h1>";
    echo "<p>Here you can manage custom settings.</p>";
}

add_action('admin_menu', 'my_custom_admin_menu');
```

✔ Creates a **new menu item in the WordPress admin sidebar**.
✔ Clicking it opens a **custom admin page**.

Adding a Submenu Under "Settings"

```
function my_custom_submenu() {
    add_submenu_page(
        'options-general.php',
        'My Submenu Page',
        'My Submenu',
```

```
        'manage_options',
        'custom-submenu-page',
        'my_custom_submenu_content'
    );
}

function my_custom_submenu_content() {
    echo "<h2>My Submenu Page</h2>";
    echo "<p>This is a submenu page under Settings.</p>";
}

add_action('admin_menu', 'my_custom_submenu');
```

✔ Adds a **submenu item under "Settings"**.

Modifying the WordPress Toolbar

The **admin toolbar (top bar)** can be **customized** to add useful links or remove unnecessary items.

Adding a Custom Toolbar Link

```
function my_custom_toolbar_link($wp_admin_bar) {
    $args = array(
        'id'    => 'custom_link',
        'title' => 'My Custom Link',
        'href'  => 'https://example.com',
        'meta'  => array('target' => '_blank')
    );
    $wp_admin_bar->add_node($args);
}

add_action('admin_bar_menu', 'my_custom_toolbar_link', 100);
```

✔ Adds a **custom link** to the WordPress admin toolbar.

Removing Default Toolbar Items

```
function my_remove_admin_bar_items($wp_admin_bar) {
    $wp_admin_bar->remove_node('wp-logo'); // Removes the WordPress logo
    $wp_admin_bar->remove_node('updates'); // Removes the updates icon
}

add_action('admin_bar_menu', 'my_remove_admin_bar_items', 999);
```

✔ **Removes unnecessary admin toolbar items**.

Customizing the Login Page

You can **customize the WordPress login page** to match your brand.

Changing the Login Logo

```
function my_custom_login_logo() {
    echo '
    <style>
        #login h1 a {
            background-image: url("https://example.com/logo.png");
            background-size: contain;
            width: 200px;
            height: 100px;
        }
    </style>';
}

add_action('login_head', 'my_custom_login_logo');
```

✔ Replaces the **default WordPress logo** with a **custom logo**.

Changing the Login URL

By default, clicking the login logo redirects to **WordPress.org**. You can **change this to your homepage**:

```
function my_custom_login_url() {
    return home_url();
}

add_filter('login_headerurl', 'my_custom_login_url');
```

✔ Clicking the logo **redirects users to your website's homepage**.

Best Practices for Extending the Dashboard

✔ **Only add what is necessary** – Avoid cluttering the dashboard with unnecessary widgets.
✔ **Use role-based permissions** – Ensure only **admins** see custom dashboard items (`manage_options`).
✔ **Use hooks (`wp_dashboard_setup`, `admin_menu`)** to keep modifications modular.
✔ **Ensure consistency** – Match the WordPress admin UI style.
✔ **Minimize dependencies** – Avoid adding external scripts unless required.

Summary

Extending the **WordPress Dashboard** allows for a **customized admin experience**.

✔ **Dashboard Widgets** – Add custom information panels using `wp_add_dashboard_widget()`.
✔ **Admin Menus & Submenus** – Create **custom admin pages** for settings and reports.
✔ **Admin Toolbar** – Modify or remove toolbar items using `admin_bar_menu`.
✔ **Login Page Customization** – Change **logos, URLs, and branding**.

By implementing **these techniques**, you can **optimize the WordPress admin area** for better usability and enhanced workflows.

Working with WP-CLI for Automation

WP-CLI (WordPress Command Line Interface) is a powerful tool that allows developers to **manage WordPress sites directly from the command line**. It enables **faster, automated workflows** for tasks like installing WordPress, managing plugins, users, and even performing database migrations.

In this chapter, you will learn:

- How to **install and configure WP-CLI**
- Basic **WP-CLI commands** for WordPress management
- Automating tasks like **theme/plugin management and database updates**
- How to **write custom WP-CLI commands**
- Best practices for **using WP-CLI efficiently**

By the end of this chapter, you will be able to **automate WordPress development** and **reduce manual overhead** with WP-CLI.

Installing and Configuring WP-CLI

1. Checking WP-CLI Installation

Most WordPress hosting environments **support WP-CLI by default**. To check if it's installed, run:

```
wp --info
```

If WP-CLI is not installed, follow the steps below.

2. Installing WP-CLI

For **Linux/macOS**, run:

```
curl -O https://raw.githubusercontent.com/wp-cli/builds/gh-pages/phar/wp-cli.phar
chmod +x wp-cli.phar
sudo mv wp-cli.phar /usr/local/bin/wp
```

For **Windows**, install via **Composer** or use **a packaged .bat file**.

After installation, verify it works:

```
wp --info
```

✔ If successful, WP-CLI is now installed.

Basic WP-CLI Commands

Once WP-CLI is installed, you can use it to **manage a WordPress site** from the command line.

1. Installing WordPress

```
wp core download
wp config create --dbname=wp_db --dbuser=root --dbpass=yourpassword
wp db create
wp core install --url="example.com" --title="My Site" --admin_user="admin"
--admin_password="admin123" --admin_email="admin@example.com"
```

✔ Installs WordPress **without using the browser**.

---

2. Managing Plugins

```
wp plugin install woocommerce --activate
wp plugin deactivate akismet
wp plugin delete hello
wp plugin update --all
```

✔ **Install, activate, deactivate, delete, and update plugins** instantly.

---

3. Managing Themes

```
wp theme install astra --activate
wp theme update --all
wp theme delete twentytwentyone
```

✔ **Install, update, or remove themes** without opening the WordPress admin.

---

4. Managing Users

```
wp user create editoruser editor@example.com --role=editor
--user_pass=strongpassword
wp user list
wp user delete 2 --reassign=1
```

✔ **Create, list, and delete users** from the command line.

---

5. Database Management

```
wp db export backup.sql
wp db import backup.sql
wp db optimize
```

✔ **Back up, restore, and optimize the database** easily.

Automating Tasks with WP-CLI

1. Running Scheduled Tasks (Cron Jobs)

WordPress uses **WP-Cron** for scheduled tasks (e.g., publishing scheduled posts).

To manually run scheduled tasks:

```
wp cron event run --all
```

To disable WP-Cron and use **real system cron jobs** instead:

1. **Disable WP-Cron** in wp-config.php:

```
define('DISABLE_WP_CRON', true);
```

2. **Schedule a cron job on the server** (runs every 15 minutes):

```
*/15 * * * * wp cron event run --due-now
```

✔ Ensures **better performance** than default WP-Cron.

---

2. Bulk Managing Posts

```
wp post list --post_type=post
wp post delete 45
wp post update 12 --post_status=publish
```

✔ **List, delete, and update posts** programmatically.

---

3. Updating WordPress Core Automatically

To **update WordPress** and all installed plugins/themes:

```
wp core update
wp plugin update --all
wp theme update --all
```

✔ This is useful for **automated maintenance scripts**.

Writing Custom WP-CLI Commands

You can create **custom WP-CLI commands** to automate specific tasks.

1. Registering a Custom WP-CLI Command

Create a custom command inside your plugin:

```
if (!class_exists('WP_CLI')) {
    return;
}

class My_Custom_CLI_Command {
    public function hello($args, $assoc_args) {
        WP_CLI::success("Hello, WP-CLI!");
    }
}

WP_CLI::add_command('mycli hello', 'My_Custom_CLI_Command');
```

✔ Running wp mycli hello will output:

Success: Hello, WP-CLI!

---

2. Creating a Database Cleanup Command

```
if (!class_exists('WP_CLI')) {
    return;
}

class WP_CLI_Cleanup {
    public function cleanup_database() {
        global $wpdb;
        $wpdb->query("DELETE FROM {$wpdb->prefix}postmeta WHERE meta_key =
'_old_meta_key'");
        WP_CLI::success("Database cleaned successfully.");
    }
}


WP_CLI::add_command('cleanup db', 'WP_CLI_Cleanup');
```

✔ Running wp `cleanup db` will remove **unused meta fields** from the database.

Best Practices for WP-CLI

✔ **Run WP-CLI commands in the correct directory** (wp-config.php must be present).
✔ **Use --allow-root cautiously** – Running WP-CLI as root can cause permission issues.
✔ **Test commands on a staging site first** to prevent data loss.
✔ **Automate maintenance tasks** like backups, updates, and database optimizations.
✔ **Limit long-running commands** – Use nohup to prevent timeouts:

```
nohup wp db export backup.sql &
```

✔ **Schedule recurring jobs** using **cron jobs** for automated updates and backups.

Summary

WP-CLI enables **faster, automated WordPress management**, reducing the need for manual work.

✔ **Install and configure WP-CLI** to manage WordPress via the command line.
✔ **Automate routine tasks** like installing plugins, themes, and database backups.
✔ **Run and schedule WP-Cron jobs** efficiently.
✔ **Write custom WP-CLI commands** to extend WordPress functionality.
✔ **Use best practices** to avoid downtime or unintended changes.

By mastering **WP-CLI**, you can **streamline WordPress development, automate maintenance, and enhance site management** with just a few commands.

Headless WordPress: React Frontend Integration

Headless WordPress refers to **decoupling** the WordPress backend from the frontend, allowing developers to use modern JavaScript frameworks like **React, Vue, or Next.js** to display content dynamically.

In this approach:

- **WordPress serves as a backend (content management system)**, providing data via the **REST API or GraphQL**.
- **React (or another JavaScript framework) is used as the frontend**, fetching content dynamically and rendering it on the client side.

Why Use Headless WordPress?

✔ **Improved Performance** – React-powered frontends load faster with client-side rendering and caching.
✔ **Better Developer Experience** – Full control over frontend rendering, without WordPress theme limitations.
✔ **Scalability** – Enables WordPress content to be used in **mobile apps, SPAs (Single Page Applications), and PWA (Progressive Web Apps)**.
✔ **Security** – The backend is separated from the frontend, reducing the risk of **direct attacks on WordPress themes**.

In this chapter, you will learn:

- How to **set up WordPress as a headless CMS**
- How to **fetch data from the WordPress REST API**
- How to **build a React frontend that consumes WordPress content**
- How to **deploy a headless WordPress site**

Setting Up WordPress as a Headless CMS

1. Enable the WordPress REST API

WordPress **natively provides a REST API**, allowing external applications to fetch content.

To check if the REST API is active, visit:

https://yourdomain.com/wp-json/wp/v2/posts

✔ If you see **JSON output**, your REST API is enabled.

If REST API is **disabled**, enable it in `functions.php`:

```
function enable_wp_rest_api() {
    add_filter('rest_enabled', '__return_true');
}
add_action('init', 'enable_wp_rest_api');
```

---

2. Install WPGraphQL (Optional)

The **REST API** is great for fetching WordPress data, but **WPGraphQL** is a more flexible alternative for querying data efficiently.

Install WPGraphQL via WP-CLI:

```
wp plugin install wp-graphql --activate
```

Check GraphQL queries at:

https://yourdomain.com/graphql

Building a React Frontend for Headless WordPress

1. Setting Up a React Project

Create a new React app using **Vite (recommended)**:

```
npm create vite@latest my-headless-wordpress --template react
cd my-headless-wordpress
npm install
npm install axios react-router-dom
```

✔ axios will be used to fetch data from the WordPress REST API.

✔ react-router-dom will manage **routing between pages**.

---

2. Fetching WordPress Data in React

Modify src/App.js to fetch posts from WordPress:

```
import { useEffect, useState } from 'react';
import axios from 'axios';

function App() {
    const [posts, setPosts] = useState([]);

    useEffect(() => {
        axios.get('https://yourdomain.com/wp-json/wp/v2/posts')
            .then(response => setPosts(response.data))
            .catch(error => console.error("Error fetching posts", error));
    }, []);

    return (
        <div>
            <h1>Headless WordPress with React</h1>
            {posts.map(post => (
                <div key={post.id}>
                    <h2 dangerouslySetInnerHTML={{ __html: post.title.rendered }}
/>
                    <p dangerouslySetInnerHTML={{ __html: post.excerpt.rendered }}
/>
                    <a href={`/post/${post.id}`}>Read More</a>
                </div>
            ))}
        </div>
    );
```

```
}

export default App;
```

✔ This **fetches blog posts** from WordPress and displays them in React.
✔ **dangerouslySetInnerHTML** allows displaying **HTML content** safely.

---

3. Creating a Dynamic Single Post Page

Modify `src/Post.js` to display **individual post content**:

```
import { useEffect, useState } from 'react';
import { useParams } from 'react-router-dom';
import axios from 'axios';

function Post() {
    const { id } = useParams();
    const [post, setPost] = useState(null);

    useEffect(() => {
        axios.get(`https://yourdomain.com/wp-json/wp/v2/posts/${id}`)
            .then(response => setPost(response.data))
            .catch(error => console.error("Error fetching post", error));
    }, [id]);

    if (!post) return <p>Loading...</p>;

    return (
        <div>
            <h1 dangerouslySetInnerHTML={{ __html: post.title.rendered }} />
            <div dangerouslySetInnerHTML={{ __html: post.content.rendered }} />
        </div>
    );
}

export default Post;
```

✔ Fetches and displays **a single blog post** using React Router.

---

4. Adding React Router for Page Navigation

Modify `src/main.jsx`:

```
import React from 'react';
import ReactDOM from 'react-dom/client';
import { BrowserRouter as Router, Routes, Route } from 'react-router-dom';
import App from './App';
import Post from './Post';

ReactDOM.createRoot(document.getElementById('root')).render(
    <Router>
        <Routes>
            <Route path="/" element={<App />} />
            <Route path="/post/:id" element={<Post />} />
        </Routes>
```

```
    </Router>
);
```

✔ Enables **navigation between the blog homepage and individual posts**.

Deploying a Headless WordPress Site

1. Deploying the WordPress Backend

Deploy WordPress on:

✔ **Cloud Hosting** (e.g., DigitalOcean, AWS, Kinsta)
✔ **Managed WordPress Hosting** (e.g., WP Engine, SiteGround)

Ensure the **REST API is accessible** from your frontend domain.

---

2. Deploying the React Frontend

To **deploy the React app** to **Vercel**:

```
npm run build
vercel deploy
```

For **Netlify**:

```
npm install -g netlify-cli
netlify deploy
```

✔ This makes your React frontend **live and connected to WordPress**.

Best Practices for Headless WordPress

✔ **Use caching for API responses** (e.g., **Redis, WP Super Cache**).
✔ **Optimize images** using a CDN (e.g., **Cloudinary, Imgix**).
✔ **Use GraphQL for more efficient data fetching**.
✔ **Protect the REST API** from unauthorized access:

```
function restrict_wp_api_to_logged_in_users($result) {
    if (!is_user_logged_in()) {
        return new WP_Error('rest_forbidden', __('REST API restricted to
logged-in users.'));
    }
    return $result;
}
add_filter('rest_authentication_errors',
'restrict_wp_api_to_logged_in_users');
```

✔ **Use authentication for private data** (e.g., **JWT Authentication plugin**).

Summary

Headless WordPress allows developers to **leverage WordPress as a backend** while using **React for modern, high-performance frontends**.

✔ **Set up WordPress as a headless CMS** using the REST API or WPGraphQL.
✔ **Fetch WordPress data in a React app** using Axios.
✔ **Create dynamic pages** with React Router.
✔ **Deploy WordPress and React separately** for better performance.
✔ **Follow best practices** for caching, security, and API optimization.

By implementing **these techniques**, you can build **fully decoupled, scalable, and modern WordPress applications** using React.

Custom Database Tables and Queries

While WordPress provides a powerful database structure using **custom post types, taxonomies, and metadata**, sometimes you need **custom database tables** to store and retrieve specialized data efficiently.

Custom tables are useful when:

✔ **Handling complex data structures** (e.g., e-commerce orders, logs, statistics).
✔ **Optimizing performance** for high-volume queries.
✔ **Reducing dependency on wp_postmeta**, which can become bloated.
✔ **Integrating with external applications** that require structured data storage.

In this chapter, you will learn:

- How to **create and manage custom tables** in WordPress.
- How to use the **$wpdb class for secure database queries**.
- Best practices for **data validation, indexing, and optimization**.

Creating a Custom Database Table

1. Using dbDelta() to Create a Table

WordPress provides **dbDelta()**, a function that safely **creates or updates tables**.

Add this function inside your plugin's activation hook:

```
function my_plugin_create_custom_table() {
    global $wpdb;
    $table_name = $wpdb->prefix . 'custom_data';

    $charset_collate = $wpdb->get_charset_collate();

    $sql = "CREATE TABLE $table_name (
        id BIGINT(20) UNSIGNED AUTO_INCREMENT PRIMARY KEY,
        user_id BIGINT(20) UNSIGNED NOT NULL,
        data_value TEXT NOT NULL,
        created_at DATETIME DEFAULT CURRENT_TIMESTAMP
    ) $charset_collate;";

    require once ABSPATH . 'wp-admin/includes/upgrade.php';
    dbDelta($sql);
}

register_activation_hook( __FILE__, 'my_plugin_create_custom_table');
```

✔ dbDelta() ensures **safe table creation**.
✔ Uses \$wpdb->prefix to follow **WordPress table naming conventions**.
✔ created_at column uses DATETIME with CURRENT_TIMESTAMP for automatic time tracking.

Inserting Data into a Custom Table

Use the \$wpdb->insert() method for secure data insertion:

```
function my_plugin_insert_data($user_id, $data_value) {
    global $wpdb;
    $table_name = $wpdb->prefix . 'custom_data';

    $wpdb->insert(
        $table_name,
        array(
            'user_id' => $user_id,
            'data_value' => sanitize_text_field($data_value),
        ),
        array('%d', '%s') // Data format: %d = integer, %s = string
    );

    return $wpdb->insert_id;
}
```

✔ **Prepares values securely** (%d for numbers, %s for strings).

✔ **Sanitizes user input** with sanitize_text_field().

Retrieving Data from a Custom Table

To **fetch all records**, use \$wpdb->get_results():

```
function my_plugin_get_all_data() {
    global $wpdb;
    $table_name = $wpdb->prefix . 'custom_data';

    return $wpdb->get_results("SELECT * FROM $table_name ORDER BY created_at DESC", ARRAY_A);
}
```

✔ Returns an **array of results** (ARRAY_A for associative arrays).

To **fetch data for a specific user**:

```
function my_plugin_get_user_data($user_id) {
    global $wpdb;
    $table_name = $wpdb->prefix . 'custom_data';

    return $wpdb->get_results(
        $wpdb->prepare("SELECT * FROM $table_name WHERE user_id = %d", $user_id),
        ARRAY_A
    );
}
```

✔ prepare() **prevents SQL injection**.

Updating Data in a Custom Table

Use \$wpdb->update() to modify existing records:

```
function my_plugin_update_data($id, $new_value) {
    global $wpdb;
    $table_name = $wpdb->prefix . 'custom_data';

    return $wpdb->update(
        $table_name,
        array('data_value' => sanitize_text_field($new_value)),
        array('id' => $id),
        array('%s'), // Format of updated values
        array('%d')  // Format of WHERE clause values
    );
}
```

✔ Ensures **secure updates** using `prepare()`.

Deleting Data from a Custom Table

Use `\$wpdb->delete()` to remove a record safely:

```
function my_plugin_delete_data($id) {
    global $wpdb;
    $table_name = $wpdb->prefix . 'custom_data';

    return $wpdb->delete(
        $table_name,
        array('id' => $id),
        array('%d') // Format for WHERE clause
    );
}
```

✔ Ensures **secure deletion** without SQL injection risks.

Displaying Custom Table Data in the Admin Panel

To create an **admin page** displaying custom table data:

```
function my_plugin_admin_menu() {
    add_menu_page(
        'Custom Data',
        'Custom Data',
        'manage_options',
        'my-custom-data',
        'my_plugin_display_custom_data',
        'dashicons-database',
        20
    );
}

add_action('admin_menu', 'my_plugin_admin_menu');

function my_plugin_display_custom_data() {
    $data = my_plugin_get_all_data();
```

```
    echo '<h1>Custom Data Records</h1>';
    echo '<table class="widefat"><thead><tr><th>ID</th><th>User
ID</th><th>Data</th><th>Created At</th></tr></thead><tbody>';

    foreach ($data as $row) {
        echo
"<tr><td>{$row['id']}</td><td>{$row['user_id']}</td><td>{$row['data_value']}</
td><td>{$row['created_at']}</td></tr>";
    }

    echo '</tbody></table>';
}
```

✔ Creates a **new admin menu item**.
✔ Displays **custom database records** in a table format.

Best Practices for Custom Database Tables

✔ **Always use \\$wpdb->prepare()** for security against SQL injection.
✔ **Index frequently queried columns** (user_id, created_at) for performance.
✔ **Avoid storing large amounts of data in a single row**—normalize data properly.
✔ **Use dbDelta() for table creation** to prevent accidental data loss.
✔ **Implement caching** for frequent queries using transients:

```
function my_plugin_get_cached_data() {
    $data = get_transient('my_plugin_data_cache');

    if (!$data) {
        $data = my_plugin_get_all_data();
        set_transient('my_plugin_data_cache', $data, HOUR_IN_SECONDS);
    }

    return $data;
}
```

✔ **Use scheduled cleanups** to prevent database bloat:

```
function my_plugin_cleanup_old_data() {
    global $wpdb;
    $table_name = $wpdb->prefix . 'custom_data';

    $wpdb->query("DELETE FROM $table_name WHERE created_at < NOW() - INTERVAL
1 YEAR");
}

if (!wp_next_scheduled('my_plugin_cleanup_cron')) {
    wp_schedule_event(time(), 'daily', 'my_plugin_cleanup_cron');
}

add_action('my_plugin_cleanup_cron', 'my_plugin_cleanup_old_data');
```

✔ Deletes **old records automatically** every day.

Summary

Custom database tables allow **efficient data storage** beyond WordPress's default schema.

✔ **Use dbDelta()** to create custom tables safely.
✔ **Insert, retrieve, update, and delete records** securely with \$wpdb.
✔ **Implement caching and indexing** to optimize performance.
✔ **Display data in the WordPress admin** for better management.
✔ **Schedule automated cleanup** to prevent unnecessary database bloat.

By following **these best practices**, you can **enhance WordPress plugins and themes with structured, high-performance data management**.

Section 6:
Best Practices for Professional Workflows

Code Organization: OOP vs. Procedural PHP

When developing WordPress themes and plugins, choosing the right approach to **code organization** is crucial for **maintainability, scalability, and performance**.

There are two primary coding paradigms used in WordPress development:

1. **Procedural PHP** – A traditional approach where functions are written in a sequential manner.
2. **Object-Oriented Programming (OOP)** – A modular approach that organizes code into reusable classes and objects.

Each approach has its **advantages and trade-offs**, and in this chapter, we will explore:

- **Differences between procedural PHP and OOP.**
- **Best practices for structuring WordPress plugins and themes.**
- **When to use procedural code vs. OOP.**
- **How to refactor procedural code into OOP for better maintainability.**

By the end of this chapter, you will be able to **write cleaner, more scalable WordPress code** using the best approach for your project.

Understanding Procedural PHP

Procedural programming is the **simplest form of PHP development**, where code is written as **a series of functions** that execute sequentially.

Example: Procedural Approach in a Plugin

```php
// Define a function to register a custom post type
function register_custom_post_type() {
    register_post_type('book', array(
        'labels' => array(
            'name' => __('Books'),
            'singular_name' => __('Book'),
        ),
        'public' => true,
        'has_archive' => true,
        'supports' => array('title', 'editor', 'thumbnail'),
    ));
}

// Hook the function into WordPress
add_action('init', 'register_custom_post_type');
```

✔ Simple and easy to understand.
✔ Works well for **small projects** and **one-time scripts**.

✗ Can become **hard to manage** in large-scale projects.
✗ **Function name conflicts** can occur if functions are not prefixed properly.

Understanding Object-Oriented Programming (OOP)

OOP (Object-Oriented Programming) is a method of organizing code into **classes and objects**, allowing for **better modularity and reusability**.

Key Concepts in OOP

✔ **Classes** – Define **blueprints** for objects.
✔ **Objects** – Instances of a class that contain **properties (variables)** and **methods (functions)**.
✔ **Encapsulation** – Keeps code **self-contained** and **modular**.
✔ **Inheritance** – Allows classes to **reuse code** from a parent class.
✔ **Abstraction** – Hides implementation details to keep code **clean and readable**.

Example: OOP Approach for Registering a Custom Post Type

```
class CustomPostType {
    private $post_type;

    public function __construct($post_type) {
        $this->post_type = $post_type;
        add_action('init', array($this, 'register_post_type'));
    }

    public function register_post_type() {
        register_post_type($this->post_type, array(
            'labels' => array(
                'name' => ucfirst($this->post_type) . 's',
                'singular_name' => ucfirst($this->post_type),
            ),
            'public' => true,
            'has_archive' => true,
            'supports' => array('title', 'editor', 'thumbnail'),
        ));
    }
}

// Instantiate the class
new CustomPostType('book');
```

✔ **Encapsulated** – The logic is inside a **class**, reducing global function clutter.
✔ **Reusable** – We can create multiple post types easily:

```
new CustomPostType('movie');
new CustomPostType('album');
```

✔ **Better maintainability** – Updates to the logic only need to be made in one place.

When to Use Procedural vs. OOP in WordPress

Scenario	Use Procedural	Use OOP
Small, simple plugins or themes	■	✗
Complex plugins or frameworks	✗	■
Reusable components (widgets, blocks, APIs)	✗	■
Database interactions & queries	✗	■
Short scripts with minimal logic	■	✗

✔ **Use procedural PHP** for **simple scripts** where OOP would add unnecessary complexity.
✔ **Use OOP** when **building structured plugins, themes, or frameworks** that require scalability.

Converting Procedural Code to OOP

Example: Procedural Code for Adding Admin Menus

```php
function my_plugin_admin_menu() {
    add_menu_page('My Plugin', 'My Plugin', 'manage_options', 'my-plugin',
'my_plugin_page');
}

function my_plugin_page() {
    echo "<h1>Welcome to My Plugin</h1>";
}

add_action('admin_menu', 'my_plugin_admin_menu');
```

Refactored OOP Version

```php
class MyPlugin {
    public function __construct() {
        add_action('admin_menu', array($this, 'add_admin_menu'));
    }

    public function add_admin_menu() {
        add_menu_page('My Plugin', 'My Plugin', 'manage_options', 'my-plugin',
array($this, 'display_plugin_page'));
    }

    public function display_plugin_page() {
        echo "<h1>Welcome to My Plugin</h1>";
    }
}

// Instantiate the class
```

```
new MyPlugin();
```

✔ **Encapsulated and reusable**.
✔ **Prevents function name conflicts**.
✔ **Easier to manage** as the plugin grows.

Best Practices for Organizing OOP Code in WordPress

1. Use a Singleton Pattern for Plugins

Ensure **only one instance** of a class is created:

```
class MyPlugin {
    private static $instance = null;

    private function __construct() {
        add_action('init', array($this, 'plugin_init'));
    }

    public static function get_instance() {
        if (self::$instance == null) {
            self::$instance = new self();
        }
        return self::$instance;
    }

    public function plugin_init() {
        // Plugin initialization logic
    }
}

// Instantiate plugin
MyPlugin::get_instance();
```

✔ **Prevents multiple instances of the plugin from loading**.

---

2. Autoload Classes with Composer

Use Composer's autoloader instead of manually including files:

```
{
    "autoload": {
        "psr-4": {
            "MyPlugin\\": "includes/"
        }
    }
}
```

Run:

```
composer dump-autoload
```

✔ **Automatically loads classes** when needed, improving performance.

3. Follow WordPress Coding Standards

Use **camelCase for functions** inside classes and **snake_case for procedural functions**:

```
class MyClass {
    public function getUserData() { }
}
function get_user_data() { }
```

✔ **Consistent coding style** improves readability.

4. Separate Concerns Using Different Classes

Use **separate classes** for different functionalities:

- `class Settings.php` – Handles plugin settings.
- `class Shortcodes.php` – Registers shortcodes.
- `class Widgets.php` – Registers widgets.
- `class API.php` – Manages API integrations.

✔ **Keeps code structured and maintainable.**

Summary

Both **procedural PHP and OOP** have their place in WordPress development.

✔ **Use procedural PHP** for small, simple plugins and quick scripts.
✔ **Use OOP** for structured, scalable, and reusable code.
✔ **Encapsulate logic inside classes** to prevent conflicts and improve maintainability.
✔ **Follow best practices** like the Singleton pattern, Composer autoloading, and separation of concerns.

By adopting **proper code organization techniques**, you can write **professional, maintainable, and scalable WordPress themes and plugins**.

Writing Maintainable and Scalable Code

Maintainable and scalable code is **easy to read, modify, and extend**. Whether you are building a theme or a plugin, writing clean, structured code ensures **long-term stability, easier debugging, and collaboration with other developers**.

In this chapter, we will cover:

- **Principles of maintainable WordPress development**
- **Best practices for writing scalable PHP, JavaScript, and CSS**
- **Using coding standards and linters**
- **Modularizing code for flexibility and reuse**
- **Documenting code for better collaboration**

By implementing **these best practices**, you will create **robust, future-proof WordPress projects**.

Principles of Maintainable Code

Maintainable code follows these principles:

✔ **Readability** – The code should be **self-explanatory** with meaningful variable names and comments.
✔ **Reusability** – Functions and classes should be **modular** and reusable.
✔ **Consistency** – Use **standardized coding styles** across your project.
✔ **Scalability** – The code should be **optimized for performance** and **future growth**.
✔ **Security** – Follow **best security practices** to prevent vulnerabilities.

A poorly written WordPress plugin or theme **can break easily**, cause **security issues**, and be **hard to update**. By following structured guidelines, you ensure **stability and long-term usability**.

Best Practices for PHP in WordPress

1. Follow WordPress Coding Standards

WordPress has an official **PHP coding standard** that all professional developers should follow.

Use Proper Naming Conventions

```
// Bad Naming
function x12func() {}

// Good Naming
function get_user_profile_data() {}
```

✔ Use **clear, descriptive function names**.
✔ Prefix **custom functions** to avoid conflicts.

Use WordPress-Specific Functions

Instead of writing raw SQL queries, use **$wpdb** and **WordPress functions** for compatibility and security.

```
global $wpdb;
$results = $wpdb->get_results("SELECT * FROM {$wpdb->prefix}posts WHERE post_status = 'publish'");
```

✔ Uses **WordPress's \\$wpdb class**, which automatically adds table prefixes.

✔ **Avoids direct database manipulation** unless necessary.

---

2. Modularize Code Using Functions and Classes

Instead of writing all logic in a single file, break it into **separate functions and classes**.

Example: Avoiding Code Duplication

Bad Approach (Repeated Code)

```
function create_custom_post_book() {
    register_post_type('book', ['public' => true]);
}

function create_custom_post_movie() {
    register_post_type('movie', ['public' => true]);
}
```

Good Approach (Reusable Function)

```
function create_custom_post_type($type) {
    register_post_type($type, ['public' => true]);
}

// Call function for multiple post types
create_custom_post_type('book');
create_custom_post_type('movie');
```

✔ **Reduces redundancy** by reusing functions.

---

3. Avoid Using Global Variables

Instead of using **global variables**, use **WordPress hooks, options, or classes** to store and retrieve data.

Bad Practice (Using Global Variables)

```
global $my_variable;
$my_variable = "Some Value";
```

Good Practice (Using WordPress Options API)

```
update_option('my_plugin_setting', 'Some Value');
$value = get_option('my_plugin_setting');
```

✔ **Uses built-in WordPress APIs**, making code **more portable** and **less error-prone**.

Best Practices for JavaScript in WordPress

1. Use `wp_enqueue_script()` for Loading JS

Never include JavaScript **inline in PHP files**. Instead, enqueue scripts properly.

Bad Practice (Inline Script in PHP)

```
echo "<script>console.log('Hello');</script>";
```

Good Practice (Using Enqueue Function)

```
function my_plugin_enqueue_scripts() {
    wp_enqueue_script('my-script', plugin_dir_url(__FILE__) . 'js/script.js',
array('jquery'), '1.0', true);
}
add_action('wp_enqueue_scripts', 'my_plugin_enqueue_scripts');
```

✔ Loads scripts in **the correct order** and ensures compatibility.

---

2. Use Event Delegation for Performance

Instead of adding event listeners to **each individual element**, use **event delegation** for better performance.

Bad Approach (Inefficient Event Binding)

```
document.querySelectorAll('.my-button').forEach(button => {
    button.addEventListener('click', () => alert('Clicked!'));
});
```

Good Approach (Event Delegation)

```
document.addEventListener('click', function(event) {
    if (event.target.classList.contains('my-button')) {
        alert('Clicked!');
    }
});
```

✔ **Improves performance** by reducing **multiple event bindings**.

Best Practices for CSS in WordPress

1. Use `wp_enqueue_style()` Instead of Inline CSS

```
function my_plugin_enqueue_styles() {
    wp_enqueue_style('my-style', plugin_dir_url(__FILE__) . 'css/style.css');
}
add_action('wp_enqueue_scripts', 'my_plugin_enqueue_styles');
```

✔ **Prevents conflicts with other stylesheets**.
✔ **Ensures proper caching and loading order**.

---

2. Use BEM (Block-Element-Modifier) for CSS Naming

BEM (Block-Element-Modifier) improves **CSS readability and maintainability**.

Bad CSS Naming

```css
.header-title { font-size: 24px; }
.header-subtitle { font-size: 18px; }
```

Good CSS Naming (Using BEM)

```css
.header__title { font-size: 24px; }
.header__subtitle { font-size: 18px; }
```

✔ **Prevents class name conflicts** and makes CSS **more structured**.

Using Linters and Code Formatters

Linters help **automate coding standard checks**. Use these tools to keep code clean:

✔ **PHP CodeSniffer** – Enforce WordPress PHP coding standards:

```
composer require squizlabs/php_codesniffer --dev
vendor/bin/phpcs --standard=WordPress plugin-folder/
```

✔ **ESLint** – Ensure JavaScript follows best practices:

```
npm install eslint --save-dev
npx eslint --init
```

✔ **Prettier** – Auto-format CSS and JavaScript:

```
npm install --save-dev prettier
npx prettier --write "src/**/*.js"
```

✔ **Stylelint** – Ensure clean CSS:

```
npm install --save-dev stylelint
npx stylelint "src/**/*.css"
```

Documenting Your Code

Writing **clear documentation** makes it easier for **other developers (and your future self)** to understand the code.

1. Use PHPDoc for Functions and Classes

```php
/**
 * Register a custom post type.
 *
 * @param string $type The post type slug.
 */
function create_custom_post_type($type) {
    register_post_type($type, ['public' => true]);
}
```

✔ **Provides function descriptions, parameters, and return values**.

2. Use README Files

Every plugin or theme should have a README.md file with:

✔ **Installation instructions**
✔ **Usage examples**
✔ **Changelog and updates**

Summary

Maintainable and scalable code **reduces bugs, improves performance, and makes collaboration easier**.

✔ **Follow WordPress coding standards** for PHP, JavaScript, and CSS.
✔ **Use reusable functions and classes** to avoid redundancy.
✔ **Use wp_enqueue_script() and wp_enqueue_style()** for assets.
✔ **Leverage linters and formatters** to automate coding style enforcement.
✔ **Document your code** with PHPDoc and README files.

By implementing these **best practices**, your WordPress projects will be **professional, scalable, and future-proof**.

Implementing WordPress Security Hardening

WordPress powers **over 40% of all websites**, making it a common target for **hackers, malware, and brute force attacks**. While WordPress is inherently secure, poor configurations, outdated plugins, and weak passwords can expose a site to vulnerabilities.

Security hardening refers to **proactive measures** that **reduce risks, protect sensitive data, and prevent unauthorized access**.

In this chapter, we will cover:

- **Common security threats in WordPress**
- **Best practices for securing themes and plugins**
- **Protecting WordPress admin and user accounts**
- **Hardening file permissions and database security**
- **Using security plugins and monitoring tools**

By implementing **these security best practices**, you will protect WordPress sites from common exploits and attacks.

Common WordPress Security Threats

Understanding security risks helps prevent attacks. The most common threats include:

✔ **Brute Force Attacks** – Hackers attempt to guess admin passwords using automated bots.
✔ **SQL Injection (SQLi)** – Attackers manipulate database queries to steal or modify data.
✔ **Cross-Site Scripting (XSS)** – Malicious scripts are injected into input fields or URLs.
✔ **Malware & Backdoors** – Unauthorized files that allow hackers to control a site.
✔ **DDoS Attacks** – Flooding a site with traffic, causing it to slow down or crash.
✔ **File Inclusion Vulnerabilities** – Attackers exploit poorly coded themes/plugins to access sensitive files.

By following security hardening techniques, we can **mitigate these risks**.

Securing WordPress Admin and User Accounts

1. Change the Default "Admin" Username

The default "admin" username is a **prime target** for brute force attacks. Change it by:

1. Creating a **new administrator account**.
2. Assigning the new account to **Administrator role**.
3. Deleting the **default "admin"** account.

Alternatively, change it via **phpMyAdmin**:

```
UPDATE wp_users SET user_login = 'newadminuser' WHERE user_login = 'admin';
```

✔ **Reduces brute force attack risks**.

---

2. Use Strong Passwords

Use **strong passwords** with a mix of **uppercase, lowercase, numbers, and special characters**.

■ Example: Z!@9aG48\$h@kP3

Use a **password manager** (LastPass, Bitwarden) to store secure passwords.

✔ **Enforce strong passwords** using a plugin like **iThemes Security** or **Wordfence**.

---

3. Implement Two-Factor Authentication (2FA)

2FA **adds an extra layer of security** by requiring a one-time verification code.

✔ Install the **Google Authenticator plugin**.
✔ Enable **2FA for all administrators and editors**.
✔ Use **email or SMS-based authentication** for additional security.

✔ **Prevents unauthorized logins even if passwords are compromised**.

---

4. Limit Login Attempts

By default, WordPress **allows unlimited login attempts**, making it vulnerable to **brute force attacks**.

To limit login attempts:

✔ Install **Limit Login Attempts Reloaded** plugin.
✔ Set a limit (e.g., **5 failed attempts** before a temporary lockout).
✔ Enable **IP blocking** after multiple failed logins.

✔ **Stops automated bot attacks** trying to guess passwords.

Hardening File and Database Security

1. Set Proper File Permissions

Use the correct **file and directory permissions** to prevent unauthorized modifications.

File/Folder	Recommended Permission
wp-config.php	400 or 440
wp-content/	755
wp-admin/	755
wp-includes/	755
themes/plugins	755
uploads	755

✔ Use **SSH or FTP** to set permissions:

```
chmod 400 wp-config.php
```

```
chmod -R 755 wp-content/
```

✔ **Prevents unauthorized access to critical files**.

---

2. Disable Directory Browsing

Hackers can access **theme/plugin directories** if browsing is enabled.

To disable it, **add this line to .htaccess**:

```
Options -Indexes
```

✔ **Prevents directory listings and unauthorized file access**.

---

3. Secure wp-config.php

The wp-config.php file contains **database credentials** and **sensitive configuration settings**.

Move it to a Non-Public Directory

WordPress allows moving wp-config.php **one directory above the root** for better security.

1. **Move the file** from:

   /public_html/wp-config.php

   To:

   /home/user/wp-config.php

2. WordPress will automatically detect it.

✔ **Prevents attackers from accessing sensitive data**.

---

4. Change the WordPress Database Prefix

By default, WordPress uses wp_ as the table prefix, making it easier for hackers to **target database tables**.

To change it:

1. Edit **wp-config.php**:

```
\$table_prefix = 'wpsecure_';
```

2. Rename tables using phpMyAdmin or WP-CLI:

```
RENAME TABLE wp_posts TO wpsecure_posts;
```

✔ **Makes SQL injection attacks harder**.

Securing Themes and Plugins

1. Keep WordPress, Plugins, and Themes Updated

✔ **Outdated plugins and themes** are the biggest security risks.
✔ Enable **automatic updates** for minor WordPress releases.

To enable automatic updates, add this to `wp-config.php`:

```
define('WP_AUTO_UPDATE_CORE', true);
```

✔ **Reduces vulnerabilities** caused by outdated code.

---

2. Install Only Trusted Plugins and Themes

✔ Download plugins and themes **only from trusted sources** (WordPress.org, Envato, official vendor sites).
✔ Avoid **nulled themes** (pirated themes often contain malware).

Use the **Wordfence or Sucuri Scanner** plugin to check for **malicious code** in themes and plugins.

✔ **Prevents installation of compromised or insecure extensions**.

---

3. Remove Unused Plugins and Themes

✔ **Deactivate and delete** plugins/themes **that are no longer used**.
✔ Check the plugin/theme's **last update date**—avoid using ones that haven't been updated for years.

✔ **Reduces the risk of outdated and vulnerable code**.

Monitoring and Security Plugins

1. Install a Security Plugin

The best security plugins for **monitoring and preventing attacks**:

✔ **Wordfence** – Firewall, malware scanning, and login protection.
✔ **iThemes Security** – Two-factor authentication, brute force protection.
✔ **Sucuri Security** – Real-time security activity auditing.

✔ **Enables security monitoring without manual effort**.

---

2. Monitor Login Activity and File Changes

Use plugins like **WP Activity Log** to track:

✔ **User logins** (who logged in and from where).
✔ **File modifications** (detects unauthorized file changes).
✔ **Failed login attempts** (to detect brute force attacks).

✔ **Helps in early detection of suspicious activity**.

3. Enable Firewall and IP Blocking

A **firewall** blocks malicious traffic **before it reaches WordPress**.

✔ Use **Cloudflare** or **Wordfence Firewall** to:
✔ Block **malicious bots and IPs**.
✔ Prevent **DDoS attacks**.
✔ Add **country-based access restrictions** if necessary.

✔ **Protects against attacks before they reach WordPress.**

Summary

Security hardening is essential to **prevent hacks, data breaches, and downtime**.

✔ **Secure the WordPress admin area** with strong passwords, 2FA, and limited login attempts.
✔ **Harden file and database security** by setting proper permissions, securing `wp-config.php`, and changing the table prefix.
✔ **Keep themes, plugins, and WordPress core updated** to prevent vulnerabilities.
✔ **Use security plugins (Wordfence, iThemes Security) to monitor and block attacks**.
✔ **Implement a firewall and activity logging** to detect suspicious activity early.

By applying **these best practices**, your WordPress site will be **fortified against security threats**, ensuring long-term stability and protection.

Performance Optimization: Caching and CDNs

Performance optimization is essential for **fast load times, better user experience, and improved SEO rankings**. A slow WordPress site can lead to **higher bounce rates** and **lost revenue**.

Two of the most effective performance strategies are:

✔ **Caching** – Temporarily storing data to reduce server load and improve response times.
✔ **Content Delivery Networks (CDNs)** – Distributing static assets across multiple locations for faster access worldwide.

In this chapter, we will cover:

- The **importance of caching** and how it speeds up WordPress.
- Types of **caching (page, object, opcode, and browser caching)**.
- How **CDNs work** and why they are essential for global performance.
- Best practices for **optimizing database queries, assets, and scripts**.

By the end of this chapter, you will have a **fully optimized WordPress site** that loads fast and performs efficiently.

The Role of Caching in WordPress

Caching **reduces server processing time** by storing pre-generated data for quick retrieval.

Without caching:

1. A visitor requests a page.
2. WordPress **retrieves data** from the database.
3. WordPress **processes PHP and executes queries**.
4. The **final HTML page is generated and displayed**.

With caching:
✔ The first request is processed as usual.
✔ The generated **HTML is stored** in a cache.
✔ Future requests **load instantly** from the cache **without processing PHP or database queries**.

Types of Caching in WordPress

Caching Type	How It Works	Example Tools
Page Cache	Stores fully rendered HTML pages	WP Rocket, W3 Total Cache, WP Super Cache
Object Cache	Stores database query results in memory	Redis, Memcached, Object Cache Pro
Opcode Cache	Caches compiled PHP code	OPcache (built into PHP)
Browser Cache	Stores static assets in the visitor's browser	`.htaccess`, Cache-Control headers

Each type plays a role in **reducing load times and improving efficiency**.

Implementing Page Caching

1. Use a Caching Plugin

The easiest way to enable caching in WordPress is by using a plugin:

✔ **WP Rocket** (Best premium caching plugin – simple and powerful).
✔ **W3 Total Cache** (Highly configurable but requires fine-tuning).
✔ **WP Super Cache** (Beginner-friendly option by Automattic).

After installation:

1. Enable **Page Cache** – This caches full HTML pages for faster delivery.
2. Enable **Browser Cache** – Forces browsers to store static files (CSS, JS, images).
3. Enable **Gzip Compression** – Reduces file sizes before sending them to visitors.

✔ **Speeds up site rendering by reducing server load**.

Implementing Object Caching

Object caching **stores database query results** so WordPress doesn't repeatedly execute the same queries.

1. Enable Object Caching with Redis or Memcached

1. Install **Redis Object Cache** or **Memcached** plugin.
2. Add this to wp-config.php:

```
define('WP_CACHE', true);
define('WP_REDIS_HOST', '127.0.0.1');
define('WP_REDIS_PORT', 6379);
```

3. Restart Redis:

```
sudo service redis-server restart
```

✔ **Reduces repeated database queries** and speeds up complex WordPress pages.

Implementing Opcode Caching

Opcode caching stores **compiled PHP code** in memory, reducing CPU load.

1. Enable OPcache (Built into PHP)

1. Check if OPcache is enabled:

```
php -i | grep opcache
```

2. If not enabled, add this to php.ini:

```
opcache.enable=1
opcache.memory_consumption=128
opcache.max_accelerated_files=10000
opcache.validate_timestamps=1
```

3. Restart PHP:

```
sudo service php-fpm restart
```

✔ **Caches PHP scripts, reducing processing time for every page load**.

Configuring Browser Caching

Browser caching allows static files (CSS, JS, images) to be **stored locally on the visitor's device**, reducing requests to the server.

1. Enable Browser Caching via `.htaccess`

Add this to your `.htaccess` file:

```
<IfModule mod_expires.c>
  ExpiresActive On
  ExpiresByType image/jpg "access plus 1 year"
  ExpiresByType image/jpeg "access plus 1 year"
  ExpiresByType image/png "access plus 1 year"
  ExpiresByType image/gif "access plus 1 year"
  ExpiresByType text/css "access plus 1 month"
  ExpiresByType application/javascript "access plus 1 month"
</IfModule>
```

✔ **Tells browsers to cache assets, reducing repeated downloads**.

Optimizing Performance with CDNs

A **Content Delivery Network (CDN)** speeds up websites by **distributing assets across multiple data centers worldwide**.

Without a CDN:
✔ A visitor in **Asia** loads your website from a **US server**, causing **high latency**.

With a CDN:
✔ The same visitor loads the site **from a server in Asia**, reducing load times.

Best CDNs for WordPress

✔ **Cloudflare** – Free + premium plans, DDoS protection, global caching.
✔ **BunnyCDN** – Affordable, excellent for media-heavy sites.
✔ **StackPath** – Good for high-performance WordPress caching.
✔ **Amazon CloudFront** – Scalable CDN for enterprise sites.

1. Configuring Cloudflare CDN

1. **Sign up at** cloudflare.com.
2. **Add your website** and update DNS records.
3. **Enable CDN & caching** settings:
   - Enable **"Auto Minify"** for CSS, JS, and HTML.
   - Enable **"Brotli Compression"** for faster file delivery.
   - Use **"Full (Strict) SSL"** to secure traffic.

✔ **Cloudflare caches assets globally, reducing server load and improving speed**.

Additional Performance Optimization Tips

1. Optimize Database Queries

Over time, WordPress databases collect **unnecessary data** like post revisions and transients.

✔ Use **WP-Optimize** to clean up:

- **Spam comments**
- **Old post revisions**
- **Expired transients**

To clean up manually via WP-CLI:

```
wp db optimize
```

✔ **Keeps your database lightweight and efficient**.

---

2. Minify and Combine CSS/JS Files

Minification removes **unnecessary characters** from CSS and JS files to reduce file size.

✔ Use **Autoptimize** or **WP Rocket** to:

- **Minify CSS/JS**
- **Combine multiple CSS files into one**
- **Defer JavaScript loading**

✔ **Reduces file size and improves loading speed**.

---

3. Lazy Load Images and Videos

Lazy loading **delays loading of images and videos** until they are visible on the screen.

✔ Use **Lazy Load by WP Rocket** or **Native Lazy Load**:

```
<img src="image.jpg" loading="lazy" alt="Example">
```

✔ **Reduces initial page load time significantly**.

Summary

Optimizing WordPress with **caching and CDNs** significantly improves **speed, performance, and scalability**.

✔ **Enable page caching** with WP Rocket, W3 Total Cache, or WP Super Cache.
✔ **Use object caching** (Redis or Memcached) to store database query results.
✔ **Enable OPcache** to cache PHP scripts for faster execution.
✔ **Leverage browser caching** to store assets locally.
✔ **Integrate a CDN (Cloudflare, BunnyCDN)** to serve static content faster worldwide.

✔ **Optimize database queries** and clean up unused data.
✔ **Minify CSS/JS and lazy load images** for a faster front-end experience.

By implementing these techniques, your WordPress site will load **faster, rank better in search engines, and provide an excellent user experience**.

Accessibility Standards for Themes and Plugins

Web accessibility ensures that **all users, including those with disabilities, can access and use** WordPress websites effectively. By following accessibility best practices, you improve **user experience, compliance with legal standards (WCAG, ADA), and SEO rankings**.

This chapter will cover:

- **The importance of accessibility in WordPress**
- **Key accessibility guidelines (WCAG, ADA, Section 508)**
- **Making themes and plugins accessible**
- **Testing tools for accessibility compliance**
- **Common accessibility issues and how to fix them**

By following these standards, you ensure that your WordPress themes and plugins **are inclusive and user-friendly**.

Why Accessibility Matters

✔ **Inclusivity** – Over **1 billion people worldwide** have disabilities. Accessible websites ensure they are not excluded.
✔ **Legal Compliance** – Many countries require **web accessibility compliance** (e.g., ADA in the US, WCAG globally).
✔ **SEO Benefits** – Google rewards **accessible websites** with better rankings.
✔ **Improved Usability** – Accessibility improvements **benefit all users**, not just those with disabilities.

Ignoring accessibility can lead to **poor user experience, legal penalties, and lost visitors**.

Understanding Accessibility Guidelines

Several accessibility standards exist, but **WCAG 2.1** is the most widely followed.

1. Web Content Accessibility Guidelines (WCAG)

The **WCAG (Web Content Accessibility Guidelines)** define accessibility across **four principles**:

Principle	What It Means	Example Fixes
Perceivable	Content should be visible and understandable	Use high contrast, text alternatives for images
Operable	Users should navigate with keyboard or screen readers	Ensure keyboard navigation, avoid auto-playing content
Understandable	Content should be easy to read and use	Simple language, clear labels, consistent navigation
Robust	Works with assistive technologies	Use semantic HTML, ARIA attributes

✔ **WCAG has three compliance levels**:

- A (Basic)

- AA (Recommended for most sites)
- AAA (Strictest, for government/health sites)

WordPress recommends **WCAG 2.1 AA compliance** for themes and plugins.

---

2. ADA (Americans with Disabilities Act)

The **ADA** applies to businesses and government websites, requiring them to be **accessible to people with disabilities**.

Key ADA compliance factors:
✔ Ensure **text-to-speech compatibility** (screen readers).
✔ Provide **closed captions** for videos.
✔ Avoid **color-based navigation** (e.g., using color alone to indicate success/error).
✔ Ensure **keyboard accessibility** (no mouse required).

---

3. Section 508 (US Government Standard)

For US federal agencies, **Section 508 compliance** is required:

✔ **Use accessible forms and buttons** (proper labels, descriptions).
✔ Ensure **documents (PDFs, Word) are screen-reader-friendly**.
✔ Use **semantic HTML for structure and clarity**.

Many private sector websites also follow Section 508 guidelines to avoid legal issues.

Making WordPress Themes Accessible

1. Use Semantic HTML for Better Readability

HTML should be **properly structured** to help **screen readers understand content**.

✔ **Use proper headings (<h1> to <h6>) for content structure.**
✔ **Avoid skipping heading levels (e.g., <h1> → <h3> without <h2>).**
✔ **Use <nav>, <header>, <article>, <aside> instead of <div> for layout.**

Bad Example (Non-Semantic HTML)

```
<div class="title">Welcome to My Website</div>
```

Good Example (Semantic HTML)

```
<h1>Welcome to My Website</h1>
```

✔ **Improves accessibility for screen readers and SEO.**

---

2. Ensure Keyboard Navigation Works

Some users **cannot use a mouse** and rely on **keyboard navigation (Tab, Enter, Arrow keys)**.

✔ **Ensure all interactive elements (menus, forms, buttons) are keyboard-accessible.**
✔ **Use** `:focus` **styles** for clarity when tabbing.

Example: Adding Focus Styles for Links and Buttons

```css
a:focus, button:focus {
    outline: 3px solid #ffcc00;
    background-color: #222;
}
```

✔ **Allows users to see where they are when navigating via keyboard.**

---

3. Use ARIA (Accessible Rich Internet Applications) Attributes

ARIA helps assistive technologies **understand complex UI elements**.

ARIA Attribute	Purpose	Example
`aria-label`	Adds descriptive text for screen readers	`<button aria-label="Close Modal">X</button>`
`aria-hidden="true"`	Hides decorative elements from screen readers	`<span aria-hidden="true">★</span>`
`role="alert"`	Announces important messages	`<div role="alert">Error: Invalid Email</div>`

✔ **Enhances accessibility without altering visual design.**

Making WordPress Plugins Accessible

1. Provide Alternative Text (`alt`) for Images

✔ **Every image should have descriptive alt text.**
✔ If an image is **decorative**, set `alt=" "` to skip it.

Example of Good `alt` **Text**

```html
<img src="chart.png" alt="Sales graph showing 20% increase in revenue">
```

✔ **Helps screen readers describe images to visually impaired users.**

---

2. Ensure Accessible Form Elements

✔ **Use** `<label>` **for all form fields** (instead of placeholders only).
✔ **Group related fields using** `<fieldset>` **and** `<legend>`.

Bad Example (No Labels, Poor Accessibility)

```
<input type="text" placeholder="Enter Name">
```

Good Example (Proper Labels)

```
<label for="name">Your Name:</label>
<input type="text" id="name">
```

✔ **Ensures forms are easy to understand and navigate.**

---

3. Avoid Auto-Playing Content

Auto-playing **audio, video, or sliders** can be **disorienting** for users with disabilities.

✔ **Allow users to control playback manually.**
✔ **Use autoplay="false" for videos.**

```
<video controls autoplay="false">
    <source src="video.mp4" type="video/mp4">
</video>
```

✔ **Prevents unwanted distractions for users with cognitive disabilities.**

Testing Accessibility in WordPress

Use the following tools to **test accessibility compliance**:

✔ **WAVE** (wave.webaim.org) – Scans for WCAG issues.
✔ **Lighthouse (Chrome DevTools)** – Audits for accessibility.
✔ **axe DevTools** – Finds and fixes accessibility issues.
✔ **NVDA (Windows) or VoiceOver (Mac)** – Test screen reader usability.

Common Accessibility Issues and Fixes

Issue	Fix
Low contrast text	Use a **high contrast ratio** (e.g., dark text on light background),
Missing alt attributes	Ensure all images have descriptive **alt text**.
No keyboard navigation	Test with Tab and **add focus styles** for elements.
Improper heading structure	Use **sequential headings (H1 → H2 → H3)**, no skipping.
Unlabeled form fields	Add **explicit <label> elements** for inputs.

Summary

Making WordPress themes and plugins accessible benefits **everyone**, not just users with disabilities.

✔ **Follow WCAG 2.1 AA guidelines** for accessibility compliance.

✔ **Use semantic HTML** (`<h1>`, `<nav>`, `<aside>`) to structure content properly.

✔ **Ensure keyboard navigation works** with `Tab`, `Enter`, and `Arrow` keys.

✔ **Add ARIA attributes** (`aria-label`, `role`, `aria-hidden`) for screen reader users.

✔ **Test accessibility using WAVE, Lighthouse, and screen readers**.

By following these best practices, your WordPress projects will be **inclusive, legally compliant, and user-friendly**.

Documenting Your Code for Collaboration

Good documentation is the foundation of **efficient team collaboration and long-term code maintainability**. Whether you are developing themes or plugins for WordPress, **clear and structured documentation helps developers understand, use, and extend your work**.

In this chapter, we will cover:

- **Why documentation is important in WordPress development**
- **Best practices for writing maintainable code comments**
- **Creating structured documentation for themes and plugins**
- **Using README files and inline comments**
- **Generating API documentation for WordPress projects**

By implementing **proper documentation techniques**, your code will be **easier to read, debug, and scale**—ensuring seamless collaboration with other developers.

Why Code Documentation Matters

✔ **Makes code easier to understand** – Saves time for future developers (including yourself).
✔ **Speeds up debugging and troubleshooting** – Helps identify logic faster.
✔ **Improves teamwork and onboarding** – New developers can quickly grasp the project.
✔ **Ensures consistency in WordPress projects** – Avoids redundancy and miscommunication.
✔ **Facilitates plugin and theme maintenance** – Reduces the risk of breaking functionality.

Without documentation, even **well-written code can become difficult to maintain** over time.

Best Practices for Inline Comments

Inline comments **explain specific parts of the code** to help other developers understand its purpose.

✔ Use **clear and concise** comments—don't explain what is obvious.
✔ Keep comments **up to date**—remove outdated information.
✔ Follow **PHPDoc standards** for structured documentation.

1. Single-Line Comments (/ /)

Use **single-line comments** for short explanations inside functions.

```
// Get the current user ID
$current_user_id = get_current_user_id();
```

✔ **Quickly explains why a line of code exists.**

---

2. Multi-Line Comments (/* ... */)

Use **multi-line comments** for **longer explanations** inside functions or logic blocks.

```
/*
 * Check if the current user is an admin.
 * This prevents unauthorized access to settings pages.
```

```
 */
if ( current_user_can( 'manage_options' ) ) {
    // Show admin settings
}
```

✔ **Documents logic blocks for better readability**.

---

3. PHPDoc for Functions and Classes

PHPDoc is the **standard commenting format** for PHP, providing **detailed explanations** of functions, parameters, and return values.

Example: PHPDoc for a Function

```
/**
 * Get the total number of posts for a given post type.
 *
 * @param string $post_type The post type slug.
 * @return int Total number of posts.
 */
function get_total_posts( $post_type ) {
    $query = new WP_Query( array( 'post_type' => $post_type ) );
    return $query->found_posts;
}
```

✔ **Clearly explains what the function does, its parameters, and return values**.

Example: PHPDoc for a Class

```
/**
 * Class Custom_Settings
 *
 * Handles custom settings for the theme.
 */
class Custom_Settings {

    /**
     * Initialize settings.
     */
    public function __construct() {
        add_action( 'admin_menu', array( $this, 'add_settings_page' ) );
    }

    /**
     * Adds a custom settings page in the WordPress admin.
     */
    public function add_settings_page() {
        add_options_page(
            'Custom Settings',
            'Custom Settings',
            'manage_options',
            'custom-settings',
            array( $this, 'render_settings_page' )
        );
```

```
     }
}
```

✔ **Helps developers understand class behavior and function responsibilities**.

Documenting WordPress Themes

1. Use a Properly Structured `style.css` Header

Every WordPress theme **requires a properly formatted header** in `style.css`:

```
/*
Theme Name: My Custom Theme
Theme URI: https://example.com
Author: John Doe
Author URI: https://example.com
Description: A custom WordPress theme built for professionals.
Version: 1.0
License: GNU General Public License v2 or later
License URI: https://www.gnu.org/licenses/gpl-2.0.html
Text Domain: my-custom-theme
*/
```

✔ **Ensures WordPress recognizes the theme correctly**.

---

2. Create a `README.md` for Theme Documentation

A **README.md** file explains **how to install, customize, and use the theme**.

Example README for a Theme

```
# My Custom Theme

## Installation
1. Download the theme ZIP file.
2. Go to **Appearance > Themes** in WordPress.
3. Click **Upload Theme** and upload the ZIP file.
4. Activate the theme.

## Customization
- Navigate to **Appearance > Customize** for theme options.
- Use `header.php`, `footer.php`, and `style.css` for modifications.

## Requirements
- WordPress 5.8+
- PHP 7.4+
```

✔ **Provides clear installation and usage instructions**.

Documenting WordPress Plugins

1. Include a `README.txt` **in Plugins**

All WordPress plugins require a **README.txt** file with plugin details.

Example README for a Plugin

```
=== Plugin Name ===
Contributors: johndoe
Tags: custom plugin, WordPress
Requires at least: 5.8
Tested up to: 6.1
Requires PHP: 7.4
License: GPL-2.0+
License URI: https://www.gnu.org/licenses/gpl-2.0.html

== Description ==
A simple plugin that adds custom functionality to WordPress.

== Installation ==
1. Upload the plugin to `/wp-content/plugins/`.
2. Activate the plugin from the **Plugins** menu.

== Changelog ==
= 1.0 =
* Initial release.
```

✔ **Ensures the plugin is properly recognized by WordPress and users.**

Generating API Documentation

1. Use phpDocumentor for Automated Documentation

phpDocumentor **automatically generates HTML documentation** from PHPDoc comments.

Installing phpDocumentor

```
composer require --dev phpdocumentor/phpdocumentor
```

Generating Documentation

```
vendor/bin/phpdoc -d src/ -t docs/
```

✔ **Creates professional API documentation for developers.**

---

2. Use WP-CLI to Document Hooks and Functions

WP-CLI allows you to **list all hooks and functions in a WordPress project**:

```
wp hook list
wp help
```

✔ **Easily documents available WordPress hooks and commands.**

Summary

Proper documentation **saves time, improves teamwork, and makes debugging easier**.

✔ **Use inline comments and PHPDoc** to describe functions and classes.
✔ **Provide structured documentation (README.md, README.txt)** for themes and plugins.
✔ **Follow WordPress coding standards** for clear and readable documentation.
✔ **Use automation tools (phpDocumentor, WP-CLI) to generate API docs**.

By documenting your code effectively, you **ensure your WordPress projects are maintainable, scalable, and professional**.

Section 7:
Deployment and Maintenance

Migrating from Local to Live: Avoiding Common Pitfalls

Developing a WordPress site locally provides a **safe environment for testing and building** without affecting a live website. However, migrating from **local development to a live server** requires careful planning to prevent **broken links, missing files, database errors, and downtime**.

In this chapter, we will cover:

- **Why proper migration is essential**
- **Pre-migration checklist**
- **Methods for migrating WordPress (manual and automated tools)**
- **Handling database updates and URL replacements**
- **Common migration issues and how to fix them**

By following **these best practices**, you can **seamlessly move your WordPress site from local to live** while avoiding downtime and errors.

Why Proper Migration is Important

Migrating a WordPress site incorrectly can result in:

✔ **Broken images and missing files** due to incorrect paths.
✔ **Database connection errors** if credentials are misconfigured.
✔ **Hardcoded local URLs not updating** to the live domain.
✔ **Lost SEO rankings** if URLs or permalinks break.
✔ **Downtime or failed migrations** if done incorrectly.

To prevent these issues, follow **a structured migration approach**.

Pre-Migration Checklist

Before migrating from local to live, ensure the following:

✔ **Backup everything** – Local files and database.
✔ **Ensure the live server meets WordPress requirements** (PHP 7.4+, MySQL 5.7+).
✔ **Disable caching and security plugins** to avoid conflicts.
✔ **Check permalink settings** – Ensure they match between local and live.
✔ **Update all plugins and themes** before migration.

Once these steps are complete, choose a **migration method**.

Methods for Migrating WordPress

1. Manual Migration (Best for Full Control)

Step 1: Export the Local Database

1. Open **phpMyAdmin** in your local development environment.
2. Select your WordPress database.
3. Click **Export** → Select **Quick export** → **SQL format** → Click **Go**.
4. Save the `.sql` file on your computer.

Step 2: Upload WordPress Files to the Live Server

1. Connect to the live server using **FTP (FileZilla, Cyberduck)** or **cPanel File Manager**.
2. Upload all files from your local **WordPress folder** to the **public_html** directory (or appropriate folder).

Step 3: Import the Database to the Live Server

1. Open **phpMyAdmin** on the live server.
2. Create a **new database** (or use an existing one).
3. Go to **Import**, select your `.sql` file, and click **Go**.

Step 4: Update the Database with the Live URL

The local database contains URLs pointing to `http://localhost`. We need to **replace these with the live domain**.

Run this SQL command in **phpMyAdmin** (replace yourwebsite.com with your actual domain):

```
UPDATE wp_options SET option_value = replace(option_value, 'http://localhost',
'https://yourwebsite.com') WHERE option_name = 'siteurl' OR option_name =
'home';

UPDATE wp_posts SET guid = replace(guid, 'http://localhost',
'https://yourwebsite.com');

UPDATE wp_postmeta SET meta_value = replace(meta_value, 'http://localhost',
'https://yourwebsite.com');

UPDATE wp_usermeta SET meta_value = replace(meta_value, 'http://localhost',
'https://yourwebsite.com');
```

✔ **Ensures all links and media files use the correct live URL.**

Step 5: Update wp-config.php with Live Database Credentials

Edit the `wp-config.php` file to match your **live database credentials**:

```
define('DB_NAME', 'your_live_database');
define('DB_USER', 'your_live_db_user');
```

```
define('DB_PASSWORD', 'your_live_db_password');
define('DB_HOST', 'localhost');
```

✔ **Ensures WordPress connects to the correct database.**

Step 6: Fix Permalinks

1. Log in to **WordPress Admin** on the live site.
2. Go to **Settings > Permalinks**.
3. Click **Save Changes** to refresh the permalink structure.

✔ **Prevents 404 errors from incorrect post URLs.**

---

2. Using a Migration Plugin (Easier & Faster)

Migration plugins **simplify the process by automating file and database transfers**.

Best WordPress Migration Plugins

✔ **All-in-One WP Migration** – Simple drag-and-drop migration.
✔ **Duplicator** – Creates a package of your entire site for easy transfer.
✔ **WP Migrate DB Pro** – Ideal for developers migrating databases.

Using All-in-One WP Migration

1. **Install the plugin** on both local and live WordPress.
2. On the **local site**, go to **Export > File**.
3. Download the exported file.
4. On the **live site**, go to **Import** and upload the file.
5. The plugin will **automatically replace URLs and database settings**.

✔ **Fast, reliable, and beginner-friendly.**

Post-Migration Steps

1. Test Everything on the Live Site

✔ **Check all pages and links** – Ensure no broken images or 404 errors.
✔ **Test forms, contact pages, and plugins** – Ensure they function correctly.
✔ **Check for missing CSS or JS files** – Inspect the browser console for errors.
✔ **Verify mobile responsiveness** – Test the site on different devices.

---

2. Enable Caching and Security

Now that the site is live:

✔ **Enable caching plugins (WP Rocket, W3 Total Cache)** for performance.
✔ **Activate security plugins (Wordfence, Sucuri)** for protection.
✔ **Set up automatic backups** to prevent data loss.

---

3. Redirect Old URLs (If Needed)

If your local site had different URLs, **set up 301 redirects** using `.htaccess`:

```
Redirect 301 /old-page https://yourwebsite.com/new-page
```

✔ **Prevents broken links and maintains SEO rankings**.

---

4. Submit the Live Site to Google Search Console

To ensure search engines recognize the live site:

1. Go to [Google Search Console] (https://search.google.com/search-console).
2. Add your live domain and verify ownership.
3. Submit a **new sitemap** (`https://yourwebsite.com/sitemap.xml`).

✔ **Ensures proper indexing and visibility in search results**.

Common Migration Issues and Fixes

Issue	Cause	Solution
"Error Establishing Database Connection"	Incorrect `wp-config.php` settings	Verify **DB_NAME, DB_USER, and DB_PASSWORD**
Broken images or missing files	Incorrect file paths	Run **search & replace** on database URLs
Redirect loop (Too many redirects error)	Mixed HTTP/HTTPS	Update **WordPress URL to HTTPS**
CSS/JS not loading	Cache issues	Clear **browser & WordPress cache**
Admin login issues	Corrupt user data	Reset password via **phpMyAdmin**

If issues persist, check **server error logs** in cPanel or use WP-CLI for troubleshooting.

Summary

Migrating WordPress from **local to live requires careful execution** to avoid common pitfalls.

✔ **Backup your local site and database** before migrating.
✔ **Use either manual migration or a migration plugin** for a seamless transfer.
✔ **Update database URLs and fix permalinks** to prevent broken links.
✔ **Enable caching, security, and backups after migration** for stability.
✔ **Test thoroughly** and submit the live site to **Google Search Console** for indexing.

By following **these best practices**, your **WordPress site will go live without errors or downtime**.

Managing Updates and Compatibility

Keeping your WordPress website **updated** is crucial for security, performance, and compatibility. WordPress frequently releases **core updates**, while themes and plugins also undergo **regular changes** to fix bugs, introduce features, and maintain security.

However, updates can sometimes break functionality if not **tested and managed properly**. In this chapter, we will cover:

- **Why updates are essential** for WordPress security and performance
- **Types of updates in WordPress (core, themes, plugins, PHP, database)**
- **Best practices for updating WordPress safely**
- **Testing updates before applying them to a live site**
- **Managing plugin and theme compatibility**

By following these guidelines, you can ensure that **updates don't cause downtime or break your website**.

Why Updates Matter

✔ **Security Enhancements** – Prevents vulnerabilities from being exploited by hackers.
✔ **Bug Fixes** – Eliminates software issues affecting functionality.
✔ **Performance Improvements** – Ensures WordPress runs efficiently.
✔ **New Features** – Keeps your website aligned with modern web standards.
✔ **Compatibility Maintenance** – Ensures themes and plugins work with the latest WordPress version.

Failing to update WordPress regularly **leaves your website vulnerable** to security threats and performance issues.

Types of WordPress Updates

WordPress updates **fall into five main categories**:

Update Type	Description	Frequency	Examples
Core Updates	Updates to WordPress itself	Monthly	New features, security patches
Theme Updates	Updates to your active theme	As needed	Bug fixes, design improvements
Plugin Updates	Updates to installed plugins	Weekly	Security fixes, new features
PHP Updates	Updates to the server's PHP version	Yearly	Performance improvements
Database Updates	Updates to WordPress database structure	Occasionally	Schema changes, optimization

Each of these updates **must be managed carefully** to avoid breaking the site.

Best Practices for Updating WordPress

1. Always Backup Before Updating

Before making **any updates**, create a **full backup** of:
✔ **WordPress files** (themes, plugins, media).
✔ **Database** (posts, pages, settings, user data).

Backup Tools:

✔ **UpdraftPlus** (Free & paid versions, automated backups).
✔ **VaultPress (Jetpack Backup)** (Reliable paid option).
✔ **WPvivid** (Full-site backups & migration).

If an update **causes issues**, you can restore the previous version **within minutes**.

---

2. Enable WordPress Auto-Updates (With Caution)

WordPress offers **auto-updates** for **core, plugins, and themes**.

Enable Auto-Updates for Core Files

WordPress **automatically installs minor security updates**, but you can enable **major updates** in wp-config.php:

```
define( 'WP_AUTO_UPDATE_CORE', true );
```

Alternatively, disable auto-updates:

```
define( 'WP_AUTO_UPDATE_CORE', false );
```

✔ **Recommended: Enable minor updates, but test major updates manually**.

---

3. Update Plugins and Themes Carefully

✔ **Check the changelog before updating** – Avoid surprises by reviewing what's changed.
✔ **Test updates on a staging site first** – Never update directly on a live site.
✔ **Update plugins one at a time** – Avoid compatibility conflicts.

How to Update Plugins Safely

1. Go to **Dashboard > Updates**.
2. Review plugin update details.
3. Update **one plugin at a time** and check the site after each update.
4. If an issue occurs, roll back using **WP Rollback** plugin.

✔ **Prevents multiple plugin conflicts from crashing your site**.

---

4. Use a Staging Environment for Testing

A **staging environment** is a **clone of your live site** used for testing.

✔ **Test updates safely before applying them to the live site**.
✔ **Identify potential issues before they affect real users**.

Ways to Set Up a Staging Site

✔ **Use a hosting provider that offers staging** (WP Engine, SiteGround, Kinsta).
✔ **Use a plugin like WP Staging** to create a local clone.
✔ **Manually set up a staging site** using a subdomain (`staging.yoursite.com`).

✔ **Avoids breaking the live website with untested updates**.

---

5. Check Plugin & Theme Compatibility Before Updating

Some plugin or theme updates may not be **fully compatible** with your version of WordPress.

How to Check Compatibility:

✔ **Read the plugin changelog** (available on the WordPress plugin page).
✔ **Check the WordPress compatibility table** (shows the last tested version).
✔ **Visit the plugin's support forum** for user-reported issues.

If a plugin **breaks** your site after updating:

✔ **Use WP Rollback** to revert to the previous version.
✔ **Disable the plugin and report issues to the developer**.

✔ **Prevents unnecessary downtime caused by plugin conflicts**.

---

6. Monitor Updates with WP-CLI

For developers, **WP-CLI (WordPress Command Line Interface)** is useful for managing updates quickly.

Check Available Updates

```
wp core check-update
wp plugin list --update=available
```

Update WordPress Core

```
wp core update
```

Update All Plugins

```
wp plugin update --all
```

✔ **Faster and more efficient for large WordPress sites**.

Common Update Issues & How to Fix Them

Issue	Cause	Solution
White screen of death (WSOD)	Plugin/theme conflicts	Disable plugins via FTP, enable WP_DEBUG

Site breaks after update	Incompatible plugin/theme	Use WP Rollback or restore backup
Database errors	Corrupt database	Run wp db repair or restore a backup
Permalinks not working	Rewrite rules changed	Resave **Settings > Permalinks**
500 Internal Server Error	PHP version mismatch	Upgrade/downgrade PHP version

✔ **Always have a recovery plan in place before updating.**

Automating Update Management

For larger WordPress sites, **automating updates** can save time while ensuring stability.

✔ **Use ManageWP or MainWP** to manage updates across multiple WordPress sites.
✔ **Set up daily backups with UpdraftPlus or Jetpack.**
✔ **Enable update notifications via email** to stay informed.

✔ **Ensures your WordPress site stays updated with minimal effort.**

Summary

Managing WordPress updates properly **prevents security risks and compatibility issues**.

✔ **Backup your site before updating** to avoid data loss.
✔ **Test updates on a staging site first** before applying them live.
✔ **Update plugins and themes carefully**—one at a time.
✔ **Monitor for compatibility issues** before updating core, plugins, and themes.
✔ **Use WP-CLI for faster update management** in developer environments.

By following these best practices, **your WordPress site will remain secure, functional, and future-proof.**

Backup Strategies and Disaster Recovery

No matter how secure or well-maintained your WordPress site is, **unexpected issues can arise**, including **hacking attempts, server failures, plugin conflicts, or accidental data loss**. A robust **backup and disaster recovery strategy** ensures that you can restore your website **quickly and efficiently** in case of an emergency.

In this chapter, we will cover:

- **Why backups are essential for WordPress sites**
- **Types of WordPress backups (file and database backups)**
- **Best backup solutions (plugins, manual methods, and hosting backups)**
- **Automating WordPress backups for security**
- **Disaster recovery: Steps to restore a WordPress site after failure**

By implementing a proper backup strategy, you can **minimize downtime and data loss, ensuring business continuity**.

Why Backups Are Essential

✔ **Protection Against Hacking** – If your site is compromised, you can **restore a clean version**.
✔ **Data Loss Prevention** – Mistakes happen, and backups provide a safety net.
✔ **Plugin and Theme Conflicts** – Updates can break your site, so **restoring a backup prevents downtime**.
✔ **Hosting Failures** – If your hosting provider has a failure, **you won't lose your site**.
✔ **Disaster Recovery** – Quickly restore your WordPress site in case of a **major incident**.

Without backups, you risk **losing valuable content, settings, and functionality**.

Types of WordPress Backups

A **complete WordPress backup** consists of:

Backup Type	What It Includes	Importance
File Backup	Themes, plugins, media, and core WordPress files	Ensures design & functionality remain intact
Database Backup	Posts, pages, users, settings, and site configurations	Restores website content and settings
Full Backup	Both **files and database**	Recommended for disaster recovery

A **full backup** is the best option for **recovering from catastrophic failures**.

Best Backup Solutions

1. Using WordPress Backup Plugins (Recommended for Ease)

Backup plugins **automate backups** and provide **easy restoration** in case of failure.

Top WordPress Backup Plugins

✔ **UpdraftPlus** – Free & premium, scheduled backups, cloud storage support.
✔ **VaultPress (Jetpack Backup)** – Real-time backups, automated restore.
✔ **BackupBuddy** – One-click full site backups & migration.
✔ **WPvivid** – Free cloud backups & migration tools.

How to Set Up Automatic Backups Using UpdraftPlus

1. Install **UpdraftPlus** from **Plugins > Add New**.
2. Go to **Settings > UpdraftPlus Backups**.
3. Click **Settings** and set up **automated daily or weekly backups**.
4. Choose a **remote storage location** (Google Drive, Dropbox, Amazon S3, etc.).
5. Click **Save Changes**.

✔ **Ensures regular backups without manual effort**.

---

2. Manual Backup via cPanel (For Full Control)

Most hosting providers offer **manual backup tools via cPanel**.

How to Manually Back Up a WordPress Site

✔ **Backup Files**

1. Log in to **cPanel**.
2. Go to **File Manager > public_html** (or WordPress root folder).
3. Select all files and compress them into a **ZIP file**.
4. Download the ZIP file to your local computer.

✔ **Backup Database**

1. Open **phpMyAdmin** in cPanel.
2. Select your WordPress database.
3. Click **Export**, choose **SQL format**, and save the file.

✔ **Ensures a full backup without relying on plugins**.

---

3. Server-Level Backups (Provided by Hosting Providers)

Many hosting companies offer **built-in automated backups**.

✔ **SiteGround** – Free daily backups for all plans.
✔ **Kinsta** – Daily & hourly backups with easy restore.
✔ **WP Engine** – Automatic daily backups with 1-click recovery.

✔ **Best for users who want hassle-free backups without additional plugins**.

Automating WordPress Backups

To **avoid data loss**, configure an **automatic backup schedule**:

Backup Frequency	Recommended For
Daily	Active blogs, eCommerce stores, membership sites
Weekly	Business websites with occasional updates
Monthly	Static sites with minimal changes

✔ **Use cloud storage (Google Drive, Dropbox, Amazon S3) to store backups securely**.

Disaster Recovery: Restoring a WordPress Site

If your website crashes, **you need a recovery plan** to restore it as quickly as possible.

Step 1: Identify the Issue

✔ **Check error messages** – Look for **PHP errors, database connection failures, or plugin conflicts**.
✔ **Review error logs** – Hosting providers store logs in **cPanel > Error Logs**.
✔ **Test on a staging site** – If possible, replicate the issue in a test environment.

Step 2: Restore the Latest Backup

Using UpdraftPlus for Recovery

1. Install **UpdraftPlus** on your WordPress site.
2. Go to **Settings > UpdraftPlus Backups**.
3. Click **Restore** and select the latest backup.
4. Choose **files, database, plugins, or themes** to restore.

✔ **Quickly restores your site in minutes**.

Manual Restoration (If WordPress is Completely Broken)

If you cannot access WordPress, restore manually:

✔ **Restore Files**

1. **Upload backup files** to `public_html` using **FTP (FileZilla)**.

✔ **Restore Database**

1. Open **phpMyAdmin** > Select database > Click **Import**.
2. Choose the **latest SQL backup** and import.

✔ **Update wp-config.php**

1. Open **wp-config.php** in File Manager.
2. Check **database credentials** (DB_NAME, DB_USER, DB_PASSWORD).

✔ **Ensures full site recovery even if WordPress is completely broken**.

Step 3: Fix Common Issues After Recovery

Issue	Cause	Solution
White screen of death (WSOD)	Plugin/theme conflict	Disable plugins via FTP, switch to default theme
Error establishing database connection	Wrong database credentials	Verify wp-config.php settings
Broken links or missing images	Incorrect file paths	Run search & replace on database URLs
500 Internal Server Error	Corrupt .htaccess file	Delete .htaccess, reset permalinks

✔ **Testing the site after restoration ensures everything is working properly**.

Summary

A **strong backup strategy and recovery plan** is essential for WordPress site maintenance.

✔ **Set up automated backups** using **UpdraftPlus, VaultPress, or WPvivid**.
✔ **Use cloud storage (Google Drive, Dropbox, Amazon S3) for secure backups**.
✔ **Test backups regularly** to ensure they can be restored.
✔ **Know how to restore WordPress manually** in case of a severe crash.
✔ **Troubleshoot common recovery issues** using error logs and FTP.

By following these best practices, you **ensure that your WordPress site remains resilient and recoverable** in any situation.

Monitoring and Scaling WordPress

A WordPress site that runs smoothly today **may struggle as traffic grows, plugins expand, or hosting limits are reached**. Monitoring performance, identifying bottlenecks, and implementing **scalability strategies** are essential to **keeping your site fast, secure, and reliable**.

In this chapter, we will cover:

- **Why monitoring is crucial for WordPress performance**
- **Essential tools for monitoring uptime, performance, and security**
- **Scaling WordPress to handle increasing traffic**
- **Optimizing database, caching, and server configurations**
- **Ensuring scalability for high-traffic sites**

By the end of this chapter, you'll have a clear strategy to **monitor and scale your WordPress site without performance drops or downtime**.

Why Monitoring WordPress is Important

✔ **Prevents unexpected downtime** – Alerts you if your site goes offline.
✔ **Detects slow-loading pages** – Improves user experience and SEO rankings.
✔ **Identifies security threats** – Detects malware and unauthorized changes.
✔ **Optimizes server resource usage** – Avoids overloading CPU, RAM, and bandwidth.
✔ **Ensures smooth scalability** – Helps WordPress handle increasing visitors without crashing.

Without monitoring, issues can go unnoticed until **they impact users and business revenue**.

Essential Monitoring Tools for WordPress

1. Uptime Monitoring (Track Site Availability)

✔ **Tool: UptimeRobot** – Notifies you if the site goes down.
✔ **Tool: Pingdom** – Checks uptime from multiple locations.
✔ **Tool: Jetpack Monitor** – Sends email alerts for downtime.

📌 **Set up alerts** so you know immediately when your site goes down.

---

2. Performance Monitoring (Track Site Speed & Load Time)

✔ **Tool: Google PageSpeed Insights** – Measures page speed & suggests improvements.
✔ **Tool: GTmetrix** – Provides in-depth load time reports.
✔ **Tool: Query Monitor** – Detects slow database queries and script issues.

📌 **Check performance weekly** and optimize slow pages.

---

3. Security Monitoring (Prevent Hacking & Malware)

✔ **Tool: Wordfence** – Firewall + malware scanner + live traffic monitoring.
✔ **Tool: Sucuri Security** – Scans for malware & hardens security.
✔ **Tool: iThemes Security** – Tracks login attempts & file changes.

📌 **Enable automated security scans** to prevent WordPress vulnerabilities.

---

4. Error Logging & Debugging (Detect PHP Errors & Conflicts)

✔ **Tool: WP Debug Log** – Captures PHP errors (`wp-config.php` setting).
✔ **Tool: New Relic** – Advanced performance & application monitoring.
✔ **Tool: Logtivity** – Tracks user actions & logs plugin errors.

📌 **Fix errors early before they break functionality**.

Scaling WordPress for High Traffic

If your WordPress site **experiences slow loading times or crashes during high traffic spikes**, it's time to **scale your website for growth**.

1. Upgrade Hosting Plan

✔ **Shared Hosting → VPS** (For medium traffic)
✔ **VPS → Dedicated Server** (For high-traffic sites)
✔ **Dedicated Server → Cloud Hosting** (For enterprise-level scalability)

📌 **Recommended Cloud Hosts for Scaling:**
✔ **Kinsta** (Google Cloud-powered)
✔ **WP Engine** (Managed WordPress scaling)
✔ **Cloudways** (Scalable cloud hosting with DigitalOcean, AWS, Google Cloud)

---

2. Implement Caching for Faster Load Times

Caching stores copies of your pages to **reduce server load**.

✔ **Page Caching:** Stores full pages for faster delivery.
✔ **Object Caching:** Caches database queries (e.g., Redis, Memcached).
✔ **Browser Caching:** Speeds up repeat visits by storing static files.

📌 **Best Caching Plugins:**
✔ **WP Rocket** – Best premium caching plugin.
✔ **W3 Total Cache** – Free, full-site caching & CDN integration.
✔ **LiteSpeed Cache** – Ideal for LiteSpeed-powered servers.

---

3. Optimize the WordPress Database

Over time, your **database accumulates unnecessary data**, which slows performance.

📌 **Use WP-Optimize to:**
✔ Clean up post revisions, spam comments, and transient options.

✔ Defragment and optimize database tables.
✔ Schedule automatic database cleanups.

---

4. Use a Content Delivery Network (CDN) for Global Speed

A CDN **delivers your website content from multiple data centers worldwide**, reducing load time for visitors in different locations.

📌 **Best CDNs for WordPress:**
✔ **Cloudflare** – Free CDN with security features.
✔ **StackPath (formerly MaxCDN)** – Faster static file delivery.
✔ **KeyCDN** – Low-cost, high-performance CDN.

---

5. Load Balancing for High-Traffic Websites

If your site receives **millions of visitors**, load balancing distributes traffic across multiple servers.

✔ **Use a Load Balancer** – AWS Elastic Load Balancer, Cloudflare Load Balancing.
✔ **Run WordPress on Multiple Servers** – Scale horizontally with multiple WordPress instances.

📌 For enterprise scaling, consider **AWS, Google Cloud, or DigitalOcean multi-server setups**.

Summary

Monitoring and scaling your WordPress site ensures **optimal performance, uptime, and security**.

✔ **Monitor uptime, performance, and security** using tools like UptimeRobot, GTmetrix, and Wordfence.
✔ **Upgrade hosting and implement caching** to handle growing traffic.
✔ **Use a CDN and optimize the database** to speed up global access.
✔ **For high-traffic sites, consider load balancing and multi-server setups**.

By following these strategies, your WordPress site will be **resilient, fast, and scalable**, even as it grows.

Contributing to the WordPress Community

WordPress is an **open-source project** that thrives on community contributions from developers, designers, writers, and users worldwide. As a professional working with WordPress, contributing to the community **not only helps improve the platform but also establishes your credibility and expertise**.

In this chapter, we will explore:

- **Why contributing to WordPress matters**
- **Ways to contribute to the WordPress ecosystem**
- **Getting involved with WordPress core development**
- **Supporting the community through documentation and forums**
- **Attending and speaking at WordPress events**

By giving back to the WordPress community, **you become part of a global network of professionals and developers shaping the future of the platform**.

Why Contributing to WordPress Matters

✔ **Gives back to the open-source project** – WordPress powers over **40% of websites**, and its development relies on community effort.
✔ **Enhances your skills** – Working with the WordPress codebase improves your coding, debugging, and problem-solving abilities.
✔ **Builds your reputation** – Contributing can help you gain recognition in the WordPress ecosystem, opening up new career opportunities.
✔ **Connects you with like-minded professionals** – The WordPress community is vast, and contributing allows you to **network with other experts**.
✔ **Improves the platform for everyone** – Your contributions help **make WordPress more secure, efficient, and feature-rich** for millions of users.

Ways to Contribute to the WordPress Ecosystem

1. Contribute to WordPress Core Development

WordPress core is **constantly evolving**, and professionals can help by:

✔ **Fixing bugs** – Reviewing and submitting patches.
✔ **Improving performance** – Optimizing queries and PHP functions.
✔ **Enhancing accessibility** – Ensuring themes and features are **usable for all users**.

How to Get Started with Core Contribution

1. **Set Up a Local Development Environment** – Install WordPress locally using **Local by Flywheel, XAMPP, or Docker**.
2. **Join WordPress Trac** – The official bug tracking and patch submission platform ([core.trac.wordpress.org] (https://core.trac.wordpress.org/)).
3. **Follow WordPress Development Blog** – Stay updated with **new releases, changes, and contribution guidelines** ([make.wordpress.org/core] (https://make.wordpress.org/core/)).
4. **Participate in Bug Scrubs** – Join WordPress core dev chats on Slack to **help review and resolve open issues**.

✔ **Contributing to WordPress Core ensures the platform remains efficient and secure.**

2. Develop and Share Free Plugins & Themes

WordPress relies on **third-party themes and plugins** for functionality and customization. By **developing and sharing your own**, you:

✔ **Help other developers and site owners** solve real-world problems.
✔ **Gain visibility in the WordPress community**.
✔ **Improve your coding skills by following best practices**.

How to Publish a Free Plugin or Theme

1. **Follow WordPress Plugin/Theme Guidelines** – Read [WordPress Plugin Developer Handbook] (https://developer.wordpress.org/plugins/) and [Theme Handbook] (https://developer.wordpress.org/themes/).
2. **Submit to the Official WordPress Repository** – Upload your theme or plugin to [wordpress.org] (https://wordpress.org/plugins/) for others to use.
3. **Maintain and Update Regularly** – Ensure compatibility with WordPress updates.

✔ **Developers who share their work get more exposure and credibility in the industry**.

3. Improve WordPress Documentation

Not all contributions require coding! **WordPress documentation is essential for helping new users and developers.**

✔ **Help write or update the WordPress Codex** ([codex.wordpress.org] (https://codex.wordpress.org/Main_Page)).
✔ **Contribute to the WordPress Developer Handbook** ([developer.wordpress.org] (https://developer.wordpress.org/)).
✔ **Improve inline code documentation in WordPress Core.**

📌 Visit [make.wordpress.org/docs] (https://make.wordpress.org/docs/) **to join the WordPress Docs Team.**

✔ **Contributing to documentation helps make WordPress more accessible and user-friendly.**

4. Help Others in WordPress Support Forums

Many beginners struggle with WordPress and need **guidance from experienced professionals**.

✔ **Answer questions on the official WordPress Support Forums** ([wordpress.org/support] (https://wordpress.org/support/)).
✔ **Provide support for plugins and themes** you develop.
✔ **Join Slack discussions** in the WordPress community.

📌 **Contributing to forums and support discussions helps grow your expertise and credibility.**

5. Participate in WordPress Events & Meetups

WordCamps and local meetups are great opportunities to network and share knowledge.

✔ **Attend WordCamps** – Annual WordPress conferences held worldwide ([wordcamp.org] (https://central.wordcamp.org/)).
✔ **Speak at Meetups** – Share insights, best practices, or case studies.
✔ **Contribute to WordPress.tv** – Record and share knowledge through **video tutorials and talks**.

📌 **Join local WordPress meetups at [meetup.com/pro/wordpress] (https://www.meetup.com/pro/wordpress/).**

✔ **WordPress events help you connect with developers, business owners, and community leaders.**

---

6. Translate WordPress for Global Accessibility

WordPress supports **multiple languages**, but many themes, plugins, and documentation still **need translation**.

✔ **Help translate WordPress Core, themes, and plugins** ([translate.wordpress.org] (https://translate.wordpress.org/)).
✔ **Ensure accessibility by translating key documentation.**

📌 **Join the WordPress Polyglots Team at [make.wordpress.org/polyglots] (https://make.wordpress.org/polyglots/).**

✔ **Translating WordPress expands its reach to non-English speaking users.**

Summary

Contributing to the WordPress community is **a rewarding way to give back** while improving your skills and professional visibility.

✔ **Developers can contribute to WordPress Core, plugins, and themes.**
✔ **Non-coders can help with documentation, translations, and community support.**
✔ **Attending and speaking at WordPress events strengthens your network.**
✔ **Helping in support forums builds your expertise and authority.**

By contributing, you **become part of the global WordPress ecosystem**, making it better for everyone.

Appendices

Appendix A: WordPress Security Checklist

Security is **a top priority for any WordPress site**, whether you're managing a personal blog, an eCommerce store, or a high-traffic enterprise site. WordPress is a **popular target for cyberattacks**, but **proper security measures** can **prevent hacking, data breaches, and downtime**.

This security checklist **covers essential security practices**, including:

✔ **Hardening WordPress login security**
✔ **Protecting your database and user data**
✔ **Securing plugins and themes**
✔ **Implementing best practices for file and server security**
✔ **Using security plugins for automated protection**

Follow this checklist to **fortify your WordPress site against threats and vulnerabilities**.

📹 1. Secure WordPress Login & User Access

✔ **Use Strong Passwords** – Ensure **admin, editor, and user passwords** are **at least 12 characters** with **uppercase, lowercase, numbers, and symbols**.
✔ **Change Default "Admin" Username** – Never use "admin" as your username; create a unique admin account.
✔ **Enable Two-Factor Authentication (2FA)** – Require users to verify login via **Google Authenticator, Authy, or SMS**.
✔ **Limit Login Attempts** – Prevent brute-force attacks with **Limit Login Attempts Reloaded** or **Wordfence**.
✔ **Disable XML-RPC** – Disable xmlrpc.php if not needed, as it is a common attack vector. Use **Disable XML-RPC** plugin.
✔ **Restrict Login Access by IP** – Restrict admin login access to specific **IP addresses** using .htaccess.
✔ **Logout Idle Users Automatically** – Use the **Inactive Logout** plugin to auto-logout inactive users.

📌 **Plugin Recommendation: Wordfence Security, Login Lockdown, Two-Factor Authentication by WP 2FA**

🔒 2. Secure WordPress Files and Directories

✔ **Set Correct File Permissions:**

- **wp-config.php** → 400 (Read-only for the owner)
- **.htaccess** → 444 (Read-only for all)
- **wp-content/uploads** → 755

✔ **Disable File Editing in WordPress Dashboard** – Prevent hackers from modifying files via **Appearance > Theme Editor** by adding this line to `wp-config.php`:

```
define('DISALLOW_FILE_EDIT', true);
```

✔ **Restrict Access to wp-config.php** – Block access using `.htaccess`:

```
<files wp-config.php>
order allow,deny
deny from all
</files>
```

✔ **Restrict Access to wp-admin Directory** – Use `.htaccess` to limit access to specific IPs:

```
<Files wp-login.php>
order deny,allow
deny from all
allow from YOUR_IP_ADDRESS
</Files>
```

✔ **Disable Directory Browsing** – Add this line to `.htaccess` to **prevent hackers from viewing sensitive directories**:

```
Options -Indexes
```

📌 **Plugin Recommendation: All In One WP Security & Firewall**

🔍 3. Secure WordPress Database

✔ **Change Database Table Prefix** – Use a **custom table prefix** instead of the default wp_ to prevent SQL injection. Change it during installation or using plugins like **WP-DBManager**.
✔ **Restrict Database User Privileges** – Ensure the WordPress database user has **only the necessary permissions** (SELECT, INSERT, UPDATE, DELETE).
✔ **Regularly Back Up Your Database** – Automate backups using **UpdraftPlus, BackupBuddy, or WP-DBManager**.
✔ **Use a Strong Database Password** – Use a **complex password** for your database to prevent unauthorized access.

📌 **Plugin Recommendation: WP-Optimize, WP-DBManager**

🚀 4. Secure Plugins and Themes

✔ **Download Only from Trusted Sources** – Avoid nulled themes/plugins and download from **WordPress.org, ThemeForest, CodeCanyon, or official developer sites**.
✔ **Update Plugins and Themes Regularly** – Outdated themes/plugins are a major **security risk**.
✔ **Delete Unused Themes and Plugins** – Remove any plugins/themes that are not in use.
✔ **Scan Plugins and Themes for Malware** – Use **Wordfence** or **MalCare** to scan for vulnerabilities.
✔ **Check Plugin Reviews & Updates Before Installing** – Avoid plugins that haven't been updated in **6+ months**.

📌 **Plugin Recommendation: Wordfence, iThemes Security, MalCare**

🛡 5. Enable Website Firewall & Malware Scanning

✔ **Use a Web Application Firewall (WAF)** – Protect your site from attacks using:

- **Cloudflare WAF** (Free & paid plans available)
- **Sucuri Web Firewall** (Premium security firewall)
  ✔ **Schedule Daily Malware Scans** – Use **Wordfence, Sucuri, or MalCare** to scan for malware and file changes.
  ✔ **Monitor Security Logs** – Track suspicious activities in **Wordfence Security > Live Traffic**.

📌 **Plugin Recommendation: Wordfence, Sucuri, MalCare Security**

⬤ 6. Secure Your Hosting Environment

✔ **Use a Secure Hosting Provider** – Choose a **WordPress-optimized hosting** with security features like **Kinsta, WP Engine, Cloudways, or SiteGround**.
✔ **Enable SSL (HTTPS)** – Install **Let's Encrypt SSL** for free or use premium SSL certificates.
✔ **Use SFTP Instead of FTP** – Always use **SFTP or SSH** instead of insecure FTP.
✔ **Enable Server-Level Firewalls** – Ensure your host provides **firewall protection and DDoS mitigation**.
✔ **Regularly Update PHP Version** – Always use **the latest supported PHP version** for performance and security.

📌 **Recommended Hosting Providers: Kinsta, WP Engine, SiteGround, Cloudways**

■ 7. Backup and Disaster Recovery Plan

✔ **Set Up Automated Backups** – Use **UpdraftPlus, BackupBuddy, or Jetpack Backups** for **daily automated backups**.
✔ **Store Backups Off-Site** – Save backups to **Google Drive, Dropbox, Amazon S3** instead of your web server.
✔ **Test Backup Restores Regularly** – Ensure backups **work correctly before an actual emergency**.

📌 **Plugin Recommendation: UpdraftPlus, VaultPress, BackupBuddy**

▮ 8. Regular Security Audits & Best Practices

✔ **Audit User Accounts** – Remove **inactive users** and enforce **role-based access controls**.
✔ **Review Security Logs Weekly** – Monitor logs in **Wordfence, Sucuri, or hosting dashboards**.
✔ **Educate Users on Security Best Practices** – Ensure all site admins **understand security basics**.
✔ **Follow WordPress Security Updates** – Stay updated via **[make.wordpress.org]** (https://make.wordpress.org/security/).

■ Final WordPress Security Checklist

Security Measure	Status
Strong passwords & 2FA enabled	■ / ✗
File permissions & .htaccess rules set	■ / ✗
Database secured with unique prefix	■ / ✗
Plugins & themes regularly updated	■ / ✗
Firewall & malware scanning active	■ / ✗
Hosting secured with SSL & SFTP	■ / ✗
Automated backups configured	■ / ✗

By following this **WordPress Security Checklist**, you **greatly reduce the risk of cyberattacks** and ensure your website remains **secure, fast, and reliable**.

Appendix B: Common Hooks (Actions & Filters) Quick Reference

Hooks are one of the **most powerful features** in WordPress, allowing developers to **extend and modify core functionality** without altering the core code. Hooks come in two types:

✔ **Actions** – Allow execution of custom code at specific points in the WordPress lifecycle.
✔ **Filters** – Allow modification of data before it is sent to the database or displayed.

This **quick reference guide** provides an overview of the **most commonly used actions and filters**, along with example implementations.

◆ 1. Understanding Actions vs. Filters

Hook Type	Purpose	Example Use
Action	Runs custom code at a specific point	Adding scripts, modifying post content, creating admin menus
Filter	Modifies data before output	Changing the title, modifying content, altering query results

Example of an Action Hook

An action hook **executes a function** at a specific point in WordPress:

```
function custom_after_post() {
    echo '<p>Thank you for reading!</p>';
}
add_action('the_content', 'custom_after_post');
```

▮ This appends a message after every post's content.

Example of a Filter Hook

A filter hook **modifies a value before it is output or saved**:

```
function custom_title_filter($title) {
    return '🔥 ' . $title; // Adds an emoji before every post title
}
add_filter('the_title', 'custom_title_filter');
```

▮ This adds a fire emoji before every post title.

◆ 2. Common Action Hooks in WordPress

Action hooks allow developers to **run functions at specific points** in the WordPress execution flow.

Theme & Frontend Actions

Hook	Purpose	Example
wp_enqueue_scripts	Enqueue styles and scripts for frontend	Load custom CSS or JavaScript
wp_head	Runs in <head> of theme	Add meta tags or tracking scripts
wp_footer	Runs before </body>	Add JavaScript at the end of the page
template_redirect	Before rendering a template	Redirect users or load a custom template
get_header	Before loading the header	Modify the header dynamically
get_footer	Before loading the footer	Modify the footer dynamically

✔ **Example – Enqueue Custom Stylesheet**

```
function load_custom_styles() {
    wp_enqueue_style('custom-style', get_stylesheet_directory_uri() .
'/custom.css');
}
add_action('wp_enqueue_scripts', 'load_custom_styles');
```

Admin Dashboard Actions

Hook	Purpose	Example
admin_menu	Add menu items in WordPress admin	Create custom admin pages
admin_init	Runs during admin page load	Register settings or scripts
admin_head	Runs inside <head> in admin	Add custom admin styles
login_enqueue_scripts	Add styles/scripts to login page	Customize login screen
save_post	Runs when a post is saved	Auto-generate metadata or log changes
user_register	Runs when a user registers	Send welcome email or assign roles

✔ **Example – Add Custom Admin Menu**

```
function custom_admin_menu() {
    add_menu_page('Custom Page', 'Custom Menu', 'manage_options',
'custom-menu', 'custom_page_callback');
}
add_action('admin_menu', 'custom_admin_menu');

function custom_page_callback() {
    echo "<h1>Welcome to Custom Admin Page</h1>";
}
```

User & Login Actions

Hook	Purpose	Example
wp_login	Fires when a user logs in	Track login activity
wp_logout	Fires when a user logs out	Redirect users on logout
user_register	Runs when a user registers	Send welcome email

✔ **Example – Redirect Users on Logout**

```
function redirect_on_logout() {
    wp_redirect(home_url());
    exit();
}
add_action('wp_logout', 'redirect_on_logout');
```

◆ 3. Common Filter Hooks in WordPress

Filter hooks allow **modification of data before it is saved or displayed**.

Content & Formatting Filters

Hook	Purpose	Example
the_title	Modify post title before display	Add prefix or suffix to titles
the_content	Modify post content before display	Add text, links, or ads
excerpt_length	Change the length of excerpts	Set custom excerpt length
excerpt_more	Modify "Read More" text in excerpts	Add custom Read More text
body_class	Modify <body> classes	Add custom classes to body tag

✔ **Example – Modify "Read More" Text**

```
function custom_excerpt_more($more) {
    return '... <a href="'. get_permalink() .'">Read More</a>';
}
add_filter('excerpt_more', 'custom_excerpt_more');
```

Query & Database Filters

Hook	Purpose	Example

pre_get_posts	Modify main query before execution	Exclude categories, modify post types
posts_orderby	Change post order in queries	Sort posts by meta value
posts_where	Modify SQL WHERE clause	Filter posts based on conditions

✔ **Example – Exclude Category from Main Query**

```
function exclude_category_from_blog($query) {
    if ($query->is_home() && $query->is_main_query()) {
        $query->set('cat', '-5'); // Exclude category ID 5
    }
}
add_action('pre_get_posts', 'exclude_category_from_blog');
```

Admin & Login Filters

Hook	Purpose	Example
login_redirect	Modify login redirection URL	Redirect users after login
admin_footer_text	Customize admin footer text	Add branding or messages
manage_posts_columns	Customize columns in post admin	Add custom post admin columns

✔ **Example – Customize Admin Footer Text**

```
function custom_admin_footer() {
    return "Custom Admin Footer - Powered by WordPress";
}
add_filter('admin_footer_text', 'custom_admin_footer');
```

◆ 4. Hook Execution Order & Priority

Hooks have **default priority 10**, but you can **adjust execution order** by setting a custom priority:

```
add_action('wp_head', 'custom_function', 15);
```

✔ **Lower priority runs first, higher priority runs later.**

◆ 5. How to Find Hooks in WordPress?

✔ Check **WordPress Developer Handbook** – [developer.wordpress.org] (https://developer.wordpress.org/reference/)
✔ Use **Query Monitor Plugin** – View hooks used on any page.
✔ Search **WordPress Core Files** – Hooks are added using do_action() or apply_filters().

◆ 6. Summary: Key Hooks for Developers

Hook	Type	Purpose
wp_enqueue_scripts	Action	Load scripts and styles
wp_head	Action	Add code to <head>
admin_menu	Action	Add custom admin pages
the_content	Filter	Modify post content
the_title	Filter	Modify post title
pre_get_posts	Filter	Modify main query

By mastering **WordPress hooks (actions & filters)**, you can **customize and extend WordPress without modifying core files**.

Appendix C: Deployment Checklist for Large-Scale Projects

Deploying a **large-scale WordPress project** requires careful planning and execution to ensure stability, security, and performance. This appendix provides a **comprehensive deployment checklist**, covering **pre-deployment, deployment, and post-deployment** best practices.

◆ 1. Pre-Deployment Checklist

Before launching your WordPress site, ensure that all essential steps are completed to prevent downtime, errors, or security vulnerabilities.

■ 1.1 Setup & Environment Preparation

☑ Ensure **development, staging, and production** environments are correctly configured.
☑ Verify **PHP, MySQL, Apache/Nginx** versions match across environments.
☑ Enable **WP_DEBUG** in staging and disable it in production.

```
define('WP_DEBUG', false);
define('WP_DEBUG_LOG', false);
define('WP_DEBUG_DISPLAY', false);
```

☑ Use **Git for version control** to track changes.
☑ Implement **SSH/SFTP access** with secure authentication.

■ 1.2 Security & Performance Optimizations

☑ Implement **SSL certificates** (Let's Encrypt or commercial SSL).
☑ Set **correct file and folder permissions**.

- Directories: 755
- Files: 644
  ☑ Restrict **XML-RPC and REST API access** if not needed.
  ☑ Install a **firewall (Cloudflare, Sucuri, or server-side)**.

■ 1.3 Database & Content Readiness

☑ Perform a **dry-run migration** in a staging environment.
☑ Optimize the database by running:

```
OPTIMIZE TABLE wp_posts, wp_options, wp_comments;
```

☑ Check for **orphaned post meta** and clean up unnecessary entries.
☑ Ensure **permalinks are set correctly** after migration.
☑ Verify **media files, uploads, and custom post types** are intact.

■ 1.4 Testing & QA Checks

☑ Test site responsiveness on **mobile, tablet, and desktop**.
☑ Perform **cross-browser testing** (Chrome, Firefox, Safari, Edge).
☑ Validate **SEO meta tags, Open Graph, and structured data**.
☑ Run performance tests using:

- **Google Lighthouse**
- **GTmetrix**
- **WebPageTest**
  - ☑ Check **error logs** for warnings or fatal errors.

✦ 2. Deployment Checklist

During deployment, follow these best practices to minimize downtime and ensure a smooth transition.

■ 2.1 Backup & Version Control

☑ Take a **full site backup** (files + database) using:

- UpdraftPlus
- VaultPress
- WP-CLI
  - ☑ Use **Git branches (staging, production)** for controlled releases.
  - ☑ Implement **.gitignore** to prevent committing sensitive files:

    wp-config.php
    /wp-content/uploads/
    /wp-content/cache/
    /node_modules/

■ 2.2 Deployment Process

☑ Use **zero-downtime deployment techniques** (e.g., Blue-Green Deployment).
☑ Deploy via **SSH & WP-CLI** to avoid file corruption.

```
wp db export backup.sql
wp plugin update --all
wp cache flush
```

☑ Push files **incrementally**, starting with **theme & plugins**, then **uploads**.
☑ Switch **staging database to production** using a tool like **WP Migrate DB**.

■ 2.3 Post-Deployment Fixes & Adjustments

☑ Run **search & replace** for domain changes in the database:

```
wp search-replace 'staging.example.com' 'www.example.com' --skip-columns=guid
```

☑ Re-save **Permalinks** (Settings > Permalinks) to refresh rewrite rules.
☑ Verify **server-side caching** is cleared (Redis, Varnish, WP Rocket).

✦ 3. Post-Deployment Checklist

After deployment, continuously monitor the site for performance issues, security risks, and content accuracy.

■ 3.1 Security & Monitoring

☑ Enable **activity logging** using **WP Security Audit Log**.
☑ Check **access logs** for suspicious activity:

```
tail -f /var/log/nginx/access.log
tail -f /var/log/nginx/error.log
```

☑ Install a **malware scanner** (Wordfence, Sucuri).
☑ Enforce **strong passwords & 2FA** for all admin users.

■ 3.2 Performance Optimization

☑ Set up a **CDN (Cloudflare, BunnyCDN, or StackPath)**.
☑ Implement **GZIP compression** and leverage browser caching:

```
gzip on;
gzip_types text/plain text/css application/json application/javascript;
```

☑ Use **lazy loading** for images & videos (`loading="lazy"`).

■ 3.3 Uptime & Analytics

☑ Set up **Uptime Monitoring** (Pingdom, New Relic).
☑ Enable **Google Analytics & Google Search Console**.
☑ Track **404 errors** and fix broken links.

◆ 4. Automation & Continuous Deployment

For large-scale projects, **automation is key** to reduce errors and improve efficiency.

■ 4.1 Use WP-CLI for Task Automation

☑ Automate **plugin & theme updates**:

```
wp plugin update --all
wp theme update --all
```

☑ Schedule **automatic database backups**:

```
wp db export /backups/db-\$(date +%F).sql
```

■ 4.2 CI/CD for WordPress Deployment

☑ Set up **GitHub Actions** or **Bitbucket Pipelines** for automatic deployment.
☑ Use **Capistrano** or **Buddy** for safe deployment workflows.
☑ Implement **rollback strategies** to restore the previous version in case of failure.

◆ 5. Summary: Deployment Best Practices

Task	Pre-Deployment	Deployment	Post-Deployment
Backup Site & Database	■	■	■

Enable Version Control (Git)	■	■	■
Test in Staging Environment	■	✕	✕
Optimize Performance & Security	■	✕	■
Enable Logging & Monitoring	✕	■	■
Automate Routine Tasks	✕	■	■

◆ 6. Final Thoughts

✔ **Thorough planning, testing, and monitoring** are critical for **successful WordPress deployments**.
✔ Utilize **automated tools & scripts** to streamline the deployment process.
✔ Keep **security, performance, and scalability** in mind for every update.

By following this **Deployment Checklist for Large-Scale Projects**, you can **ensure a stable, secure, and optimized WordPress environment**.

Appendix D: Resources for Further Learning

Mastering WordPress development is a continuous journey. With evolving technologies, new security challenges, and emerging best practices, staying up-to-date is essential for professionals. This appendix provides a curated list of **resources** to help you further your expertise in **WordPress development, theme and plugin creation, security, and performance optimization**.

◆ 1. Official WordPress Resources

The best place to start is **WordPress.org**, which provides official documentation, updates, and resources.

🔗 **[WordPress Developer Resources]** (https://developer.wordpress.org/) – Comprehensive guide to WordPress APIs, themes, and plugins.
🔗 **[WordPress Codex]** (https://codex.wordpress.org/) – Legacy documentation with tutorials and references.
🔗 **[WordPress Support Forums]** (https://wordpress.org/support/) – Community-driven Q&A for WordPress issues.
🔗 **[Make WordPress]** (https://make.wordpress.org/) – Contribute to WordPress development and discussions.
🔗 **[WordPress Plugin Repository]** (https://wordpress.org/plugins/) – Explore official plugins and source code.
🔗 **[WordPress Theme Directory]** (https://wordpress.org/themes/) – Discover and analyze theme structures.

◆ 2. Books & E-Books on WordPress Development

📕 **WordPress Plugin Development Cookbook** – Yannick Lefebvre
📕 **Professional WordPress: Design and Development** – Brad Williams, David Damstra, Hal Stern
📕 **WordPress All-in-One for Dummies** – Lisa Sabin-Wilson
📕 **WordPress: The Missing Manual** – Matthew MacDonald
📕 **Headless WordPress with React & WP REST API** – Mario Pabon

◆ 3. WordPress Development Blogs & Websites

For daily updates, tutorials, and guides, follow these **WordPress-focused blogs**:

📕 **[WP Tavern]** (https://wptavern.com/) – News, updates, and analysis on WordPress ecosystem.
📕 **[Smashing Magazine]** (https://www.smashingmagazine.com/category/wordpress/) – Advanced WordPress tutorials and design strategies.
📕 **[CSS-Tricks WordPress Section]** (https://css-tricks.com/archives/#article-header-id-10) – WordPress theming and development tips.
📕 **[Torque Magazine]** (https://torquemag.io/) – Industry trends and insights on WordPress.
📕 **[WPTuts+]** (https://code.tutsplus.com/categories/wordpress) – Plugin development, customization guides, and best practices.
📕 **[SitePoint WordPress]** (https://www.sitepoint.com/wordpress/) – Beginner to advanced guides on WordPress programming.

◆ 4. Online Courses & Training Platforms

If you prefer structured learning, these platforms offer **high-quality WordPress development courses**:

🎓 **[LinkedIn Learning (WordPress Courses)]** (https://www.linkedin.com/learning/topics/wordpress) – WordPress for beginners to advanced developers.
🎓 **[Udemy - WordPress Development Courses]** (https://www.udemy.com/courses/search/?q=wordpress%20development) – Covers custom themes, plugins, and security.
🎓 **[Codecademy - WordPress Development]** (https://www.codecademy.com/) – PHP, JavaScript, and WordPress integration courses.
🎓 **[WPCasts]** (https://wpcasts.tv/) – Video tutorials on advanced WordPress techniques.
🎓 **[Envato Tuts+ WordPress Courses]** (https://tutsplus.com/) – Courses on WordPress REST API, headless WordPress, and automation.

◆ 5. YouTube Channels for WordPress Developers

YouTube is a great **free** resource for step-by-step tutorials and live coding sessions.

▶ **[WPCrafter]** (https://www.youtube.com/c/WPCrafter) – Beginner-friendly tutorials and development tips.
▶ **[LearnWebCode]** (https://www.youtube.com/c/LearnWebCode) – WordPress theming, API, and JavaScript integration.
▶ **[Develop with WP]** (https://www.youtube.com/channel/UCwYUSXj2nGFe8f3lJpzmwvw) – Custom theme and plugin development.
▶ **[Traversy Media]** (https://www.youtube.com/c/TraversyMedia) – Covers WordPress, PHP, JavaScript, and REST APIs.
▶ **[Kinsta Academy]** (https://www.youtube.com/c/KinstaHosting) – WordPress hosting and performance optimization.

◆ 6. WordPress Performance & Security Resources

🛡 **[OWASP WordPress Security Guide]** (https://owasp.org/www-project-top-ten/) – Best practices for securing WordPress.
🛡 **[Sucuri Blog]** (https://blog.sucuri.net/) – Security vulnerabilities, malware protection, and hardening techniques.
🛡 **[Cloudflare Learning Center]** (https://www.cloudflare.com/learning/) – Web security and CDN optimization.
🛡 **[Google PageSpeed Insights]** (https://pagespeed.web.dev/) – Performance analysis and recommendations.
🛡 **[GTmetrix]** (https://gtmetrix.com/) – Speed and caching optimizations for WordPress.
🛡 **[Wordfence Blog]** (https://www.wordfence.com/blog/) – Updates on WordPress security threats and fixes.

◆ 7. WordPress Developer Tools & Frameworks

🔧 **[WP-CLI]** (https://wp-cli.org/) – Command-line interface for WordPress automation.

🔧 **[LocalWP]** (https://localwp.com/) – Local WordPress development environment.

🔧 **[Theme Check]** (https://wordpress.org/plugins/theme-check/) – Ensures themes meet WordPress coding standards.

🔧 **[Query Monitor]** (https://wordpress.org/plugins/query-monitor/) – Debugging and performance profiling tool.

🔧 **[Advanced Custom Fields]** (https://www.advancedcustomfields.com/) – Extends WordPress content management.

🔧 **[Redux Framework]** (https://redux.io/) – Extensible options framework for themes & plugins.

🔧 **[Timber]** (https://timber.github.io/docs/) – Twig templating for cleaner theme development.

🔧 **[REST API Handbook]** (https://developer.wordpress.org/rest-api/) – Official WordPress REST API documentation.

◆ 8. Community & Networking

Engaging with the WordPress community helps **expand knowledge, share solutions, and contribute to the ecosystem**.

🌐 **[WordPress Slack Community]** (https://make.wordpress.org/chat/) – Connect with developers and contributors.

🌐 **[WordCamp Events]** (https://central.wordcamp.org/) – Attend global conferences and networking meetups.

🌐 **[WordPress Stack Exchange]** (https://wordpress.stackexchange.com/) – Advanced development Q&A forum.

🌐 **[GitHub WordPress Repositories]** (https://github.com/WordPress/) – Explore open-source WordPress projects.

🌐 **[Reddit r/WordPress]** (https://www.reddit.com/r/Wordpress/) – Discussions, troubleshooting, and tips.

🌐 **[Meetup WordPress Groups]** (https://www.meetup.com/pro/wordpress/) – Find local WordPress networking events.

◆ 9. Contributing to WordPress

If you want to **give back to the WordPress community**, consider **contributing to core development, documentation, translations, and accessibility**.

💡 **[Contribute to WordPress]** (https://make.wordpress.org/) – Official WordPress contribution guide.

💡 **[Report Bugs on Trac]** (https://core.trac.wordpress.org/) – Help improve WordPress core.

💡 **[Translate WordPress]** (https://translate.wordpress.org/) – Help translate WordPress into multiple languages.

💡 **[Improve Documentation]** (https://developer.wordpress.org/) – Help maintain accurate WordPress docs.

💡 **[WordPress Accessibility Team]** (https://make.wordpress.org/accessibility/) – Contribute to making WordPress accessible for all.

Staying updated with **WordPress development, security practices, and performance techniques** ensures that you remain at the top of your game. These resources provide **comprehensive learning paths** for **beginner to advanced WordPress professionals**.

Conclusion

Congratulations! By reaching this point, you have **successfully navigated through the world of professional WordPress development**—from setting up your local environment to mastering advanced techniques for **custom themes and plugins**. You have explored critical aspects of WordPress architecture, security hardening, performance optimization, and deployment best practices.

Mastering WordPress is not just about coding—it's about **understanding the ecosystem, writing maintainable code, and delivering scalable solutions**. As a professional, your work impacts users, businesses, and the broader WordPress community.

Key Takeaways from This Book

As you move forward, here are some key lessons to keep in mind:

■ **Build with Best Practices** – Stick to WordPress coding standards, use hooks effectively, and keep your code modular.
■ **Prioritize Security** – Implement **nonces, data validation, and secure authentication** to protect your users.
■ **Optimize for Performance** – Use **caching, CDNs, and database optimization** for faster load times.
■ **Leverage Advanced Tools** – Master **WP-CLI, REST API, and headless WordPress** to build cutting-edge applications.
■ **Document and Version Control** – Keep your projects organized with **clear documentation and Git versioning**.
■ **Stay Updated & Keep Learning** – WordPress evolves constantly. Follow the **official WordPress blogs, courses, and community discussions**.

The Future of WordPress Development

The **WordPress landscape is continuously evolving** with the rise of **block-based editing (Gutenberg), full-site editing (FSE), headless CMS architectures, and AI-powered integrations**. As a professional, embracing these advancements will **give you a competitive edge** and **position you as a leader** in the WordPress development space.

Some areas to watch:
* **Headless WordPress** with React, Next.js, and GraphQL.
* **Performance-optimized themes** using modern JavaScript frameworks.
* **AI-driven personalization** for better user experiences.
* **Automation & DevOps** for seamless deployment.

Giving Back to the WordPress Community

One of the best ways to grow as a professional is **to contribute to the WordPress ecosystem**. Whether through **developing plugins, improving core features, contributing to open-source projects, or mentoring new developers**, your input helps **WordPress thrive**.

Ways to contribute:
● Join WordPress meetups and **WordCamps**.
✗ Contribute to **core development and plugin reviews**.
🐞 Write blog posts, tutorials, or **help improve documentation**.
🔍 Test beta versions and report security vulnerabilities.

Your Next Steps

Now that you have built a strong foundation, it's time to **apply what you've learned**. Consider:

🚀 **Launching Your Own Theme or Plugin** – Apply what you've learned to create a **high-quality WordPress product**.

💼 **Offering Freelance Services or WordPress Consulting** – Build a **successful business** around your WordPress expertise.

🎓 **Teaching Others** – Share your knowledge by **writing, teaching, or mentoring new developers**.

Your journey with WordPress is just beginning, and **the possibilities are endless**. Whether you're **building client projects, launching your startup, or innovating with new technologies,** your skills will **drive the future of WordPress development**.

Thank you for reading *WordPress for Professionals: Mastering Custom Themes and Plugins*. I hope this book has **empowered you to build exceptional WordPress solutions**.

Happy coding, and keep creating! 🚀

www.ingramcontent.com/pod-product-compliance
Lightning Source LLC
Chambersburg PA
CBHW080554060326
40689CB00021B/4851